WHEN THE FUTURE BEGINS

D0544360

Dedicated to my grandfather Harry Lindkvist, a futurologist decades before it became mainstream

WHEN THE FUTURE BEGINS

A Guide to Long-term Thinking

MAGNUS LINDKVIST

LONDON   MADRID
NEW YORK   MEXICO CITY
BOGOTA   BUENOS AIRES
BARCELONA   MONTERREY

DUN LAOGHAIRE-
RATHDOWN LIBRARIES
DLR20001026903
BERTRAMS 09/12/2013
£12.99
BR

www.businesspublishersroundtable.com

All rights reserved. Without limiting the rights under copyright
reserved, no part of this publication may be reproduced, stored or
introduced into a retrieval system, or transmitted, in any form or
by any means (electronic, mechanical, photocopying, recording
or otherwise), without the prior written permission of both the
copyright owners and the publisher of this book.

© Magnus Lindkvist
© LID Publishing Ltd. 2013

Printed and bound by CPI Group (UK) Ltd, Croydon, CR0 4YY

ISBN: 978-1-907794-24-7

This book contains details of products and treatments that the
author has used which he believes has greatly improved his
health and well-being. Please note, however, that the information
contained within this book does not constitute medical advice
and does not amount to a general endorsement of any product.
Anyone looking to undergo treatment of a similar kind should
consult their doctor.

Page design: e-Digital Design Ltd

CONTENTS

CHAPTER ONE
SEDUCED BY FUTURE

The F-word

We live in the future. The future of the past. But whereas the future of the past was shiny, techie, happy, with age-old conflicts resolved, the 2010s are rather muddled. Sitting on my patio in a middle-class suburb of Stockholm on a cloudless summer evening in July 2012, I am surrounded by technologies from the early 1900s onwards.

The buildings are from the late 1980s and are starting to look old. The cars parked along the street represent a random sample from the past fifteen years. The summer sky reminds me of my childhood some three decades ago. The for-home-use-only jeans I'm wearing might have been in vogue around the same time as Bon Jovi. The future looks nothing like The Future. In fact, it looks like a hodgepodge of different time periods.

My mind wanders.

In The Future, we will all live on Mars. Or some other remote part of the galaxy. Dressed in digital, iPod-white uniforms that constantly monitor our health and wellbeing, we will live until we are two hundred years old. At least. Work will be a thing of the past and instead of being paid for labour, we will be rewarded for the beauty of our thoughts. Nationalities and skin colour will be memories too as the world's gene pool converges into one single entity, a result of globalized intermarriage and cross-boundary procreation.

In The Future, we will transcribe and manipulate matter as easy as we do bits and genes today. When we need something, we make it. On demand. Doesn't matter if it's a car part or a perfect replica of a fourteenth-century battle-axe.

In The Future, poverty and starvation will merely be pages in the lesser-used domains of Wikipedia's replacement, which in turn will be chemically administered via syringe during childhood. Knowledge as vaccination.

In The Future, we will be wiser, happier, healthier and richer.

In The Future.

The three sexiest words in the world.

Sexy because what the words "In The Future" do is seduce our minds and lure them into some imaginary space where things are better than today. Or worse. A mental refuge from the tyranny of the here and now. This prison of the present.

"In The Future" is not just an escape hatch. It's also a key.

Between now and the future is a door that can only be opened if we start pondering what lies far beyond the door. Just over the threshold is tomorrow, some average Tuesday. But wandering further into the darkness, we can explore what pleasures or sorrows next summer might bring us. Or retirement. Or the retirement of our grandchildren.

"In The Future" is a drug, a mind-altering substance.

"In The Future" is a weapon. In the hands of a visionary politician or enterprising entrepreneur, these words can make converts out of sceptics.

"In The Future" has become a global pastime. In the shift from a world where most things were decided for us to one where we are condemned to a life of eternal freedom and choice, the only way to navigate is to explore what different paths might or might not bring us. And there is no right answer. How could there be? There isn't some other you running in the opposite direction, not reading these lines right now.

"In The Future" is the reason this book exists.

The meanings of a word

We use one word to group together the coming milliseconds with the next millennia. In doing so, we lose information. The coming seconds might, strictly speaking, be part of the future, but we reserve the epithet The Future to more distant times and places, whether it's the dream vacation we hope to have one day, the life our kids might lead when they have grown up and left home, or some faraway date like, say, 31 July 2048.

Masking it all with the same words hides the fact that the future is a *mille-feuille* of dates, situations, hopes, prayers, places and dreams. To think about the future is to whizz through a fraction of this multilayered universe.

"What should I do this weekend?"

"Should I save in stocks or bonds or splurge like there's no tomorrow?"

"Is climate change real?"

"Will we one day find life in outer space?"

"Will I marry?"

"Will I be happier in California?"

"When will I die?"

Like a carrot on a stick, the future is a mental construction and, like a memory, it doesn't really exist. But we can use questions like these to explore what lies beyond our immediate situation and navigate what roads, dreams and nightmares may come. In order to simplify, it's useful to think in terms of a three-dimensional cube.[i]

Clear or hazy view?

We can be quite certain of some things like our own mortality or the direction of a tennis ball being dropped, while other things are nearly impossible to know. Like knowledge itself. What will we know in the future and how will have gained this knowledge? A clear or hazy view reflects these two different vantage points that, in turn, tend to affect us in different ways. The things we can see clearly tend not to qualify as "future" but rather as laws-of-physics, facts-of-life or simple routines, whereas the things hiding in the haze are open to interpretation, mythmaking and fear.

Large or small consequence?

Consequence can be measured in many different ways. Economists would prefer to talk about utility whereas psychologists will try to assess mental effects. Moreover,

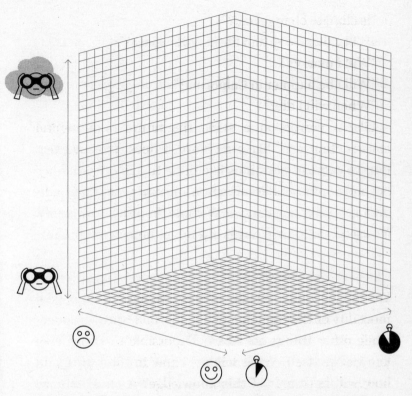

This cube represents the mental space occupied by the future. When we think about it, we journey between the different chambers inside of it.

the scope of consequence means different things to different people. A fourteen-year-old boy whose girlfriend has just dumped him will see it as the end of the world whereas the rest of the world – apart, perhaps, from his parents – will live on, oblivious to this personal disaster. Similarly, the mutation of a virus somewhere in the world right now is of minuscule consequence to begin with, but might create a catastrophic pandemic later on.

Good or bad?

Finally, there is an important distinction between things that are ultimately benign and those that tend to be negative. Again, this is a matter of subjective value judgment that tends to fluctuate over time. Think of the ideas that were once good and are now viewed as bad, like bloodletting patients to cure disease, a common medical practice up until the 1800s.

The point of the Future Cube is not to clearly delineate and evaluate every single thought or event that we will come across in a lifetime. Rather, it is to conceptualize the mental framework we use when thinking ahead. We can also use it to differentiate between future-thinking in different eras. The societal optimism felt in the US and Europe during the 1950s, for example, tended to congregate mainly in the Good and Large consequence box, whereas the pessimism we see around us in the 2010s stays firmly in the hazy and bad corner. Finally, we can also use the cube to distinguish between the ways in which different kinds of people will think about the future. Overconfident youngsters, religious zealots and rampant pessimists will often have a crystal clear view of the future, only to have it squashed once reality sets in.

What role you will play in relation to events in the cube depends on where in the cube you see the future and how you perceive your own capabilities. Many things can be altered and changed over time – even ageing. Cultural conditioning plays a big role in this. We have seen a general shift in the past century from a fatalist view –

accept life as it is – to a more omnipotent sentiment. As futurist Stewart Brand puts it: "We are as gods and might as well get good at it...".[ii]

A book about our favourite destination

In a famous experiment in the late 1980s, American students were asked to report how often they think about the future. The result was, on average, 12 percent of the participants' time or an hour out of every eight-hour working day.[iii] That might not sound like much but if you look at the statistics on how we spend our time, an hour every day is quite a lot. It has also been found that thinking about the future leads to a greater sense of happiness and wellbeing.[iv] In other words, the future is one of our favourite destinations. This book aims to take a closer look at why and how we make this mental pilgrimage to what Swedes call *framtiden*, or "forward-time", and thereby transform a place on the timeline into a mindset.

In this mission, I have chosen to sacrifice certain aspects of future-thinking.

This book is not some techno-determinist utopia about the many good things that some emergent technology will bring. Those are fun to read about but not particularly useful.

Neither is it the currently fashionable dystopian vision about a future where pollution, evil scientists and greedy businessmen have conspired to wreak havoc on this fragile planet. Those tend to be quite scary, they may make you reflect on your own (in)actions, but they don't provide you with tools to think ahead. They are, in a sense, ready-to-eat meals.

Finally, this book is not a prescriptive manual. It won't help you understand exactly how you will behave if tomorrow you won the lottery or needed to escape from a giant tidal wave.

This book is not about the actual future – it doesn't seek to compete with meteorologists, stock analysts, pundits, tarot cards, crystal orbs, science fiction novels or some other kind of entity claiming the gift of prophecy. Instead, it is an inquiry into the imagined future – our preoccupation with the word "future" – how we think and how we should think about tomorrow and beyond. I have built on the mental tools developed by future-thinkers, sci-fi writers and other predictioneers to construct a guide to long-term thinking. In its guidance, it will also point out the shortcomings and common errors we make when envisioning tomorrow, because as the philosopher Friedrich Hegel once said, "To be aware of limitations is already to be beyond them." What I hope to achieve in writing this is to inspire better, more constructive future-thinking so that you won't have to rely too much on all the future babblers out there.

When The Future Begins is built around four questions:
- What is the future?
- How do we and how should we think about the future?
- How can we change the future?

The next chapter, Chapter Two: A Future-Thinking World, will define the future and future-thinking as well as describe why it is a more important skill today than it was historically. It will also distinguish between different kinds of future.

Chapter Three: The Fine Art and Questionable Science of Predicting the Future will focus on the basics of futurology, a fancier word for future-thinking.

Chapter Four: Futurological Fallacies and Predictive Pitfalls will make you aware of the most common ways that our future-thinking brain leads us astray.

Chapter Five: How The Future Is Created takes a closer look at how we can create our way forward, rather than remaining locked into a determinist view of tomorrow.

Chapter Six: Future Friends and Future Foes is a reflection on the kind of societal forces that try to try to sway our opinions about the future.

Chapter Seven: The Eternal Promise is where it all ends. Or begins.

My assumptions about you, dear reader

A book about thinking is bound to have a number of shortcomings. We still know very little about consciousness and its intricacies. Furthermore, our thinking about thinking is changing as we are gaining insight into the brain's many secrets. Depression used to be viewed as a result of poor upbringing, but the consensus now is that it's a chemical disorder. Similarly, we might, in the future, realize that future-thinking was the result of a hormonal imbalance. For now, I have tackled this topic from a subjective perspective, building heavily upon my own experience of thinking ahead. It is my hope that you and I will share some traits in how we think. I will also make the assumption that you are a time-and-attention-challenged smart individual. You don't have time for a long-winded, philosophically intricate dictionary about futurism and its many shortcomings. Neither are you looking for some all-encompassing belief system (think cheap New Age philosophy) about tomorrow. You are not a full-time futurist or crystal ball gazer. Most of us don't sit around strategizing and predicting things all day long. We simply want to find ways of living and working a little bit better, and I wrote this book as a contribution to our everyday quest. Or should that be every day's quest?

CHAPTER TWO
A FUTURE-THINKING WORLD

"Don't just watch your feet as you walk."
Dag Hammarskjöld, former UN Secretary General

When does the future begin?

The next few seconds are 99% predictable. That's why we don't refer to them as "The Future" but reserve that epithet to more distant places. The future is the uncertainty at the point where the shortcomings of our senses need to be augmented by our thoughts. Our five senses are preoccupied with and designed for the present. Should you happen to hear voices from a long time ago or feel flavours from next week, you might be blessed with supernatural abilities but it might also be time to have your head examined.

Beyond the present, however, lie an infinite amount of possibilities. What's around the corner down the street? What will the weather be like tomorrow? What am I going to do next weekend? How will I celebrate my fiftieth birthday? When will I retire? This is a tiny snapshot of the world beyond the present. Being unable to see, hear, touch, smell or taste it, however, means that we have to rely on our brain's capacity to time travel.

Learning to time travel

My twin sons were born in 2008. The first year, as any parent of infants can attest, is a strenuous mix of feeding, diaper changing, stroller walking and sleepless nights. If babies are able to think beyond the next meal, they keep that capacity well hidden. The time-travelling brain doesn't get going until we are a few years old. We sometimes claim that children are blessed with creative skills. Alas, they are not. They lack the future-thinking capabilities residing in the prefrontal cortex of the brain as they aren't fully functioning until they are in their mid-twenties. This is why they will blurt out whatever is in their head, which is sometimes mistaken for creativity.[1]

Children will also, in the name of uninhibited spontaneity, eat snot or lick snails. Moreover, the future-thinking parts of the brain are the first to wither away, which is why you hear elderly people making remarks like "I just don't care about the future anymore, I just live in the here and now." In the short gap between our mid-twenties and early sixties, however, we can mentally fly around in time exploring what dreams, and nightmares, may come.

But when we think about the future, we don't have a limitless horizon. Instead, we tend to stay fairly close to our temporal homes in the present and not veer too far down the timeline. Hence, most of the future-probing inquiries we make will focus on events in the coming weeks or months. Occasionally, when urged to think

---

1. Incidentally, drinking a glass or two of wine has the same effect since alcohol numbs the prefrontal cortex.

long-term, it is unlikely that we make any significant effort to explore beyond, say, the year 2025. A mere decade and a half from now.

The reasons for this are fairly straightforward. Future-thinking – like many other of the brain's functions – is a survival mechanism and will thus home in on events near and far that might either threaten us or elevate our wellbeing to new levels. In business, when executives ask what a particular industry might look like in the future, they rarely do it out of curiosity. When I was asked by some managers at an automotive manufacturer what the cars of the future might be like, it was made clear during the conversation that what they were really asking was this: "How long can we keep on selling more or less the same thing without having to change too much?" In the short run, things will mainly be incremental. In the long term, mainly existential.

Why Christmas and hangovers are always unexpected

In the 1980s there was an American TV series called *The Greatest American Hero*. The series focused on a reluctant superhero whose powers were unreliable. You see, he had found a suit and he could fly and don super strength, but he wasn't in full control of these superhuman abilities, so the series became a kind of situational comedy based on failed attempts to fly and similar.

The future-thinking capabilities of the brain are a bit like *The Greatest American Hero*. We can think ahead, but the ability is somewhat half-baked. We can dream ourselves into magnificent scenarios of future happiness, yet be surprised that Christmas is only a week away now and we are yet to buy presents. Or we spend a day strategizing at a corporate conference only to drink ourselves silly in the evening and forget all about the inevitable hangover.

We are not future-thinking machines but living human beings, whose brains are sometimes full of thoughts about tomorrow but at other times are fully engaged in the present or reminiscing. We have sketchy thoughts and images interrupting our everyday life with random impulses about tomorrow. Perhaps future-tinkering is a more accurate description of what most of us succumb to. We live our lives poking around for answers and we often get anxious, perplexed, confused, angry, sad, and even suicidal when pondering what might lurk in the next year or beyond. That is why societies throughout history have gone to great lengths to make up intricate theories about what governs our fate and shapes the future.

Why future-thinking matters in a modern world

We are equally cursed and blessed with an organ that thinks about the future part-time, but biological endowment isn't the sole reason we think ahead. After all, the fact that we have reproductive capabilities doesn't necessarily explain – at least not fully – the rise of pornography. Context is what matters.

Why did human beings change their view of the future from something that was predetermined to something that could be created? What in the human condition changed to transform us from fatalists frozen in the headlights of a fixed future scenario into captains of our own fate?

The future as a concept has always played a significant role in society, or at least for as long as our species has had the mental capacity to think about it. The seven cardinal sins of the Christian faith, for example, could be seen as dire warnings about giving in to indulgences and impulses in the here and now while ignoring future consequences. In other words, the root of all evil – from sloth to gluttony – was failing to think about the future.

Similarly, politics – whether practised by elected politicians or autocratic emperors – has always been a battle not so much about the future itself but about images of what lies ahead, and how to avoid or embrace them – usually with pompous formulations like "we live in different times now" or "we are heading towards disaster" thrown in for good measure. However, the past century has brought a number of dramatic changes in how our lives are led and in how society functions. These have in turn placed greater emphasis on the need to consider long-term actions and reactions. More specifically, we can see five shifts happening over the past one hundred and fifty years.

1. From a cyclical to a progressive society

The question "What will the future be like?" only matters in a world where change is the norm. In a cyclical society, we cannot expect our children's lives to be longer or much different than our own. We can argue that the word "future" was quite meaningless up until the mid-1800s. To understand what happened, take a look the diagram opposite showing the percentage of all economic output and all years lived for each century in history going back two thousand years.

This graph[v] shows something remarkable. For centuries, there was no significant difference between the present and the future. Our children lived as long as us or less. Societies didn't become richer, and making money was basically about taking money – through taxation, plunder, gifts or sacrifice. From the first to the seventeenth century, society was, from an economic and health perspective, stagnant. Progress – the underlying principle of most societies today – did not exist.

With the rise of new ways of thinking, new governing principles, industrialism, and scientific breakthroughs,

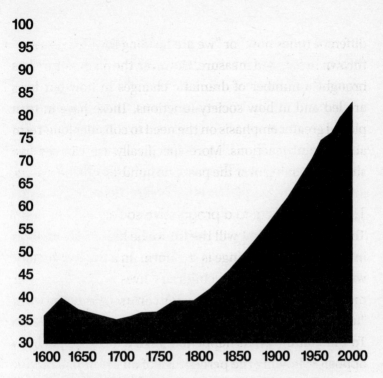

Life Expenctancy At Birth 1600–2009 (with years displayed on the x-axis and average life expectancy on the y-axis). Source: Jim Open and James W.Vaupel, *Broken Limits to Life Expectancy*.

lives changed drastically; often within a generation. This is when future-thinking moved from the ivory towers of philosophy – think Nostradamus – to more mainstream areas like popular literature and politics. In fact, the first work of futurology is considered to be Herbert George ("H.G.") Wells's book Anticipations from 1902, wherein he marvelled at the rapid change of the past few decades and speculated about what the future could bring in terms of technology, societal change and its consequences for everyday life.

2. From guided by fate to guided by chance

When doing a speaking engagement, I have to wear black Björn Borg underwear. This is a peculiar case of superstition since I consider myself somewhat rational; but I am by no means the only superstitious rationalist. Football players will touch the grass when entering a pitch for good luck. People with a fear of flying will go through some kind of ritual before boarding a flight. Hotels and airlines will avoid certain numbers in floors or seat rows. People will swallow fish oil tablets or some other placebo if it promises a long, healthy life or more illustrious skin.

These are remnants from a time when the conviction of human beings was that our lives were governed by higher forces. All we needed to do in order to thrive – or, at least, not die – was pray, repent and sacrifice the odd animal or human being to keep enslaving entities at bay. We may – as a society – have evolved from the notion that everything is predetermined, but there is still some fatalist residue on the fabric of daily living. These notions have something in common with science fiction films: they assume that the future is already out there somewhere and will strike down upon us at a specific date.

This is a top-down vision of the future, and people might still ask the question "what will happen in the future?" as if there is only one particular kind set aside for us. At the other end of the scale lies the darling of motivational speakers: the idea that the future is something we create ourselves – the bottom-up view of the future. The future not as a final destination, but as a universe of possibilities, opportunities and threats.

The humans-as-future-makers idea was so prevalent in the early 2000s that we haven't stopped to reflect on the fact that it is, in some ways, as scientifically inaccurate as its fatalistic opposite. No matter how hard you try – and entrepreneurs, politicians and motivational speakers always insist you should try hard – you cannot will a tennis ball to go sideways if you throw it up in the air. Gravity will be with us for some time yet – something that cosmetic surgeons are doubtless happy to hear – and it is just one of many forces governing our lives and futures. To say "we create our future" is seductive but, in many ways, it is as silly as saying "our future is predetermined". The reality is that the future is a mix of bottom-up and top-down conditions. Some things are preordained and should be accepted as part of the human condition. Others are open for us to challenge and change.

3. Slave to oneself

People have moved from primarily serving some greater deity – a god, a caste, ancestors, a class system, and so on – to primarily serving themselves.

Novelist Jonathan Franzen made the following observation about how fictional writing changed as we moved from a society built on duty to one built on choice:

> *The 18th century was not only the moment when fiction writers abandoned the pretense that their narratives*

weren't fictional; it was also the moment when they began taking pains to make their narratives seem not fictional— when verisimilitude became paramount. [...] When business came to depend on investment, you had to weigh various possible future outcomes; when marriages ceased to be arranged, you had to speculate on the merits of potential mates. The novel, as it was developed in the 18th century, provided its readers with a field of play that was speculative and risk free. While advertising its fictionality, it gave you protagonists who were typical enough to be experienced as possible versions of yourself and yet specific enough to remain, simultaneously, not you.[vi]

The novel shifted from being an escape vehicle to being a simulator. Simulation is the essence of future-thinking and it is only effective when we are left to our own devices about how to live our lives. However, when the choices are many and complex, we tend to outsource simulation to the experts; as we shall see in point five, Complexity.

4. The rise of choice
A starving or otherwise suffering person will not think about anything beyond immediate demands. Future-thinking is a luxury we can devote our time to when other, more basic demands have been met. My great-grandparents, living in the late 1800s, did not really have to think about what to become in life, what to study and where to settle down as these things were more or less dictated to them by their surroundings – in terms

of geography, parental guidance and the implications brought by social status. My grandparents, a few decades hence, gained a bit more freedom and had to think about where in Sweden they could see themselves living and working. They were free to date, free to marry whomever they wanted, free to choose what to study and work with. My parents – born in the 1940s – were the first real teenage rebels so they had an extended period of time of experimenting with all kinds of things.

Fast forward to my sons, both born in 2008. They live in what can best be described as a WWW-World – a World of Whatever, Whenever, Wherever. From the number of brands, media channels and lifestyles on offer while growing up to more existential dilemmas like sexuality, faith, education and relationships, they are in a sense condemned to freedom. In a world of excessive choice, future-thinking moves from being a rare luxury to an everyday necessity.

It even hides in many seemingly mundane activities. Pension saving, marriage proposals, vacation planning, job switches and even trivial tasks like ordering from a restaurant menu or choosing what queue to join in the supermarket are examples of embedded future-thinking. Likewise, the results of poor projections can be seen all around us – from divorce rates and type two diabetes to the now unused gadgets and exercise machines that were the perfect purchase or birthday present only a few months ago.

5. Complexity

In the fall of 2010, I got a chance to take a peek behind the scenes of Stockholm's International Airport Arlanda. In one of the hangars, they were servicing a Boeing 737 and I got a chance to talk to one of the mechanics. He was one of those elderly, salty raconteurs that you imagine would hang out around the harbour telling stories from decades on the seas, had this been a different century. Now, dressed in blue overalls smeared with oil stains, he took us on a tour of the aircraft. They were doing an extensive check-up and had therefore removed the walls inside the plane, exposing the intricate gadgetry and the millions of wires hiding behind the plastic panelling that the passengers see. Amazed, I proceeded to interrogate him about what the different wires were, how he could keep track of them and why – with so many things to keep track of – things didn't go wrong more often. When I asked him about the training of mechanics, he told me something profound.

"You see," he said, "when I started this job many years ago, I was allowed to work on virtually any model of any aircraft. Today, I'm only allowed to work on one. One model of one plane – the Boeing 737 800 series, the one we are currently in."

What he was saying is that aircraft manufacturing has become so complex, with so many unique parts, that airplane mechanics have to "hyperspecialize" to keep up. Airplanes aren't the only kind of machinery having gone through this metamorphosis of sorts. The diagram below shows the number of parts per machine in a number of different product categories.[vii]

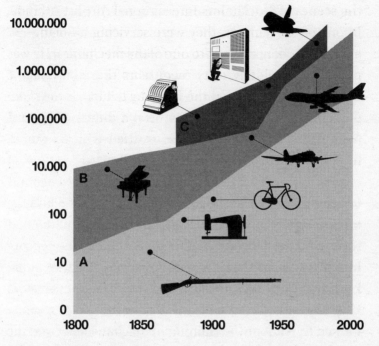

Number of parts per manufactured machine years 1800–1990. (A = Mass-produced products, B = Niche products, C = Unique products). Source: Kevin Kelly, *What Technology Wants.*

In a similar development, the number of products on offer has skyrocketed too. It's been estimated that a city the size of New York contains about ten billion[vii] stock keeping units, or SKUs for short.[2] We don't even have to go to New York. Your local supermarket is bound to contain more products and more varieties of products than your great-grandparents saw in their entire lifetime.

These developments point to a complex society and

---

2 SKU = A stock-keeping unit is a number used to identify each unique product or item for sale in a store (i.e. a medium-sized black shirt is one SKU while its XL equivalent is a different SKU and the medium-sized white shirt is a third SKU and so on).

perhaps the most complex thing of all is the amount of information we face on a daily basis. Try googling the words "how much information is there in the world?" and the results say it all. The one billion plus hits are scattered, often contradictory, and their credibility can, in many cases, be questioned. The kind of information society we live in does not necessarily empower people and lead them to new insights; instead it bewilders, frustrates and wears out attention spans. That is why we have become so reliant on experts who thrive on our confusion.

To understand things requires a lot more knowledge and training than what was required some decades back. From the intricacies of climate change to the vast intertwined bundle that is modern finance, we let highly specialized expertise make sense of these things for us. In addition, we use the future tense as a kind of antidote to our confusion. The present is turbulent, cluttered and contradictory, so we create clarity by looking ahead – just like staring at the horizon can alleviate seasickness. Climate change, the financial fate of nations and other twenty-first century topics reflect a society thinking about its future. What will happen if we lower carbon emissions versus what will happen if we don't? What will happen if the US changes tack and what happens if they don't?

When The Future(s) began

These five overlapping developments in society – progress, reason, individualism, choice and complexity – show that future-thinking was born sometime in the mid to late 1800s. However, I have used the word "future" to describe any place in time ahead of us – bar the first few seconds – but as Charles Darwin once noted, our ignorance of the laws of variation is profound. There is no such thing as "the future", only futures – plural. More specifically, there are five variations of future that we face and that, in turn, affect our thinking in different ways.

1. The slow and gradual future

Someone once said that the good thing about the future is that it arrives one day at a time. Continental drift and human ageing are two examples of snail-paced future making. These kinds of shifts tend to be quite predictable, which is the reason most politicians tend to favour demographic shifts when making bold predictions about the future. We know almost exactly how many seventy-year-olds there will be in Europe, Asia or the US in forty years' time.

Future-thinking within the slowly unfolding, predictable future is, in essence, a statistical exercise. Insurance companies make money because they – or rather their Excel sheets – know the likelihood of a 35-year-old middle-class male dying of cancer across a population. The problem occurs, however, when we lose track of these shifts because they were simply too slow. Gradualism blinds us into assuming that things have never and will never change. We talk about biological evolution, but no living human being has actually seen – and probably won't live to see – evolution in action. That's why people can make up all kinds of theories about how man was made.

Absence of evidence is mistaken for evidence of absence. Slow changes also hold the secrets as to why many good companies go bad. Howard Schulz, the founder of coffee chain Starbucks, made the following remark about why Starbucks fell on hard times in 2007: "Starbucks had begun to fail itself. Obsessed with growth, we took our eye off operations and became distracted from the core of our business. No single bad decision or tactic or person was to blame. The damage was slow and quiet, incremental, like a single loose thread that unravels a sweater inch by inch. Decision by decision, store by store, customer by customer, Starbucks was losing some of the signature traits it had been founded on."[ix]

2. The quick and unexpected future

Acclaimed filmmaker James Cameron was not acclaimed nor much of a filmmaker in the early 1980s.[x] During the making of the chronically bad B-movie *Piranha 2: The Spawning*, Cameron was afraid that the Italian producer would fire him before the movie was finished and put his own name on the film. He had, after all, done it before to other aspiring filmmakers. Cameron decided to cling on to the project. With a maxed-out credit card, he squatted in a Rome hotel and ate leftover food from room service trays left in the corridors. Bad idea. The dodgy food gave him a severe case of food poisoning and he was now cuddled up in bed with a burning fever. His dreams were feverish, almost hallucinatory.

In one of them, he was visited by a robotic skeleton walking through fire. He told his friend – film producer Gale Anne Hurd – about the dream, who he had promised to make a movie with at some point in his life, and said that he wanted to make the movie about this thing of his fever dreams, this "terminator", as he had started calling it.

The rest is movie history. The paltry budget meant that *The Terminator* couldn't be set in the future, so Cameron made it about time travel instead. It made a star out of Arnold Schwarzenegger and was not only 1984's most successful film but also one of the most profitable ever made. So what are we to make of this tale of creativity? The answer is "nothing at all". All we can deduce is that ideas come to us or, at least, to certain people. Some come in showers, some in feverish dreams. Some in states of relaxation and others when we are stressed out of our minds.

There is simply no way for us to know exactly what these ideas will be and when they will arrive. Yet they are capable of making money, satisfying consumers and even making a dent in popular culture, politics, science or the arts. These erratic, unpredictable bits of the imagination are even capable of altering the future. Many of the ideas that emerge out of the mystical darkness of creative minds will be good; they will change entire lives for the better, like penicillin, or just make fifteen-minute intermissions a bit more tolerable, like the mobile phone game "Angry Birds".

Some, however, will be bad. When the disaster preparation unit in Oslo had a scenario exercise in April 2011, they agreed that the most likely and most impactful disaster to strike Norway's capital was a flu pandemic.[xi] A terrorist strike was deemed to be of fairly low probability and impact. Three months later, Anders Behring Breivik butchered nearly a hundred people – mostly teenagers – in a combined bombing and shooting spree. "The Future is always sooner and stranger than you think", as Linkedin founder Reid Hoffman once said. For the sake of future-thinking, discontinuities are as vital to understand as the slow, gradual trends described in the previous section. Not because we will be able to predict them, but because they present the future not so much as a statistical exercise but as a challenge of the imagination.

3. The actual future

These first two kinds of future are products of the mind. We either calculate or imagine some point in time ahead of us and what it might be like. But they are nothing more than a mental image and will only remain valuable or exciting as long as they describe a time that hasn't yet come to pass. One day, however, this future date or year will be transformed into a more mundane place we call the present. "The Future" is noble, better, worse or just a lot different, but when it finally arrives on some Wednesday morning, we are reminded of all the things that didn't change or developed in the direction we predicted.

Technology often suffers from this gap between expectation and reality. When people in the 1960s imagined the year 2000, they told stories of leisure space stations, flying cars and robot butlers. Technology did certainly bring marvels like the World Wide Web, laptop computers and more fuel-efficient cars, but compared with the sci-fi urban landscapes people dreamt of, they are quite mundane. Imagined future technology is exciting, scary, beautiful and world changing. In the real world, technology is often boring, invisible and prone to the same kind of controversies, opinions and frustrations that we thought it would solve. People will likely complain about waiting in line at the Teleportation Station and the security pat-downs needed before you're beamed off to a drab office park in Slough, England.

4. The imagined future

The imagined future is, by definition, what we mean when we use the f-word since the future cannot exist in any other place than the mind. Whether logically calculated, like the number of pensioners in the year 2048, or dreamt up by a Hollywood screenwriter, the future is a place where our hopes and fears can run free, untroubled by inconveniences like facts, gravity or red tape. It is a paracosm, a parallel reality we explore to create some kind of effect; like titillate moviegoers, sway the electorate or daydream your way out of a dull meeting.

As an influential tool, using the words "in the future"

is highly effective. Past events demand that we check facts and use a language or imagery that evoke a sense of agreement and familiarity. Future-thinking, on the other hand, only needs to instil a certain feeling to be useful. We often ask historians, political pundits or experts to make predictions about tomorrow when in reality, an artist or a pep-talking sports coach might be more appropriate if the kind of future we seek is not the actual, boring kind but the spectacle we love or fear – or love to fear.

5. The future that never arrives

A hundred years is an eternity for a dragonfly but a blink of an eye for a rock. If butterflies had futurist conferences, they would speculate about what the coming three months would bring. Time is relative and we are human-centric when we think about time. A lifetime, eighty years or so, is viewed as long-term, whereas an hour is immediate.

When we envision something called "The Future", the silent agreement is that this moment is bound to fall within something we, or at least our grandchildren, will have a chance to experience. Hence, the most common dates in future-thinking are a round numbers like 2020, 2030 or 2050. A year like 4872 AD or 10334 AD is simply too distant for us to envision and wrap our minds around. As human beings, we take our own perception of time as being the norm and are thus blind to things that take thousands of years to emerge or shift, like mountains being worn down by the elements or fossilized plants turning to oil.

Why think forward?

The different kinds of future reflect the fact that there are different motives for thinking ahead. Firstly, there's the utilitarian aspect to future-thinking – the fact that we can get insights and ideas that might help us make more money or find opportunities by outlining what tomorrow's world might look like. When companies ask trendspotters and futurologists to make presentations, this is usually the kind of perspective they are interested in learning more about.

The second motivation to think and, especially, talk about is to gain influence and status. From medicine men to politicians, "the future" is an eternal well from which to dig up all kinds of images, thoughts and ideas that we can then be afraid of, quarrel about or fall in love with. The Medicine Man himself or the party of said politician usually plays a key role in preventing or accelerating the kind of future presented. The third reason people escape into the future is, well, to escape. Sometimes from yourself – summer vacation plans with their promises of a "different you" come to mind – and sometimes from the nasty, unforgiving, idiot-saturated place called The Present.

Science fiction authors were in many cases deeply troubled individuals whose reasons to write about another time were to seek refuge from the time in which they were trapped. Scientists have even found that people who think about the future a lot tend to be happier than those who do it less.

The fourth reason to think ahead is that we use the future to better understand the present. George Orwell's novel *1984* was really about the year 1948. *The Planet of The Apes* was set on Earth and annihilated by what we worried about at the time (an atom bomb in the 1970s TV series and genetic engineering in the 2011 version). The future clarifies the present by pointing to and exaggerating certain promises, hopes or fears. The fifth reason we think about the future is... well, no reason whatsoever. We just do it. Think about it. We don't ask why our hearts beat. They just do. Similarly, our ability to think far ahead in time is embedded in another body organ that wasn't exactly optional when you and I were put together.

Conclusion and next chapter

Every moment has its own unique kind of future. Every person's outlook on what lies ahead will differ in certain ways from what other people envision. What is described as a singular, definitive destination – the future – is in reality a giant kaleidoscope of ideas. The challenge we face today when we peer into this kaleidoscope is that we get little or no help in how we should think constructively about the future. If schools really wanted to prepare children for the modern world, shouldn't future-thinking be a required part of any academic curriculum? Shouldn't all politicians be forced to master the many intricacies of long-term thinking? It's like we have invented a car but have very little interest in teaching people to drive.

This opens a chasm between what is required of people today – from selecting suitable ways to save for a pension to committing to a long-term relationship – and how adept they are at mastering these challenges. The chasm creates bewilderment that in turn gives rise to superstitions, religious beliefs or other ideas that can alleviate the confusion. It is unsurprising that advisors – from spiritual guides and self-help quacks to pension planners and career counsellors – constitute one of the fastest growing sectors of the economy for the past couple of decades.

We live in a kind of middle age where we have been endowed with a magnificent capability – to think beyond the present – combined with a society that requires greater forecasting skills, but we still struggle to find the right tools that best serve us. The next chapter will begin to cover the basics of futurology – the fine art and somewhat questionable science of predicting what lies ahead.

CHAPTER THREE

THE FINE ART AND QUESTIONABLE SCIENCE OF PREDICTING THE FUTURE

"Tomorrow obeys a futurist the way lightning obeys a weatherman."
Bruce Sterling

Introduction

In the spring of 1987, a time capsule ceremony was held at the Windows On The World restaurant atop the World Trade Center's North Tower in New York City.[xii] The time capsule was full of predictions about the year 2012 – twenty-five years ahead at the time – by celebrated science fiction authors who called themselves "Writers of The Future".

The predictions ranged from the mildly amusing ("there will be little sex outside marriage" and "we will see a reaction to the women's movement. Men will demand to be portrayed by the media as the sensitive, caring creatures that they are") to the usual science fiction promises ("a network of levitated superconducting trains will be under construction in Western Europe and in Japan" and "the exploration of space is picking up speed, both by manned colonization and robot probes") to the clichéd dystopian landscapes ("AIDS will have become the leading cause of death worldwide" and "crime will have become so prevalent as to threaten the social fabric").

Some of the predictions were eerily prescient ("all storable forms of energy will be expensive. Machines will be designed to use only minimal amounts of it" and "economic collapse will have cost America its dominant world role"), but most gravitated between vague future-ramblings and pure hogwash. Future Studies – or futurology, to give it the fancier word – are concerned with "three Ps and a W":[xiii] Possible, probable or preferable futures and wildcards, defined as highly unlikely yet impactful events. The question this chapter will address is this: Does futurology work?

To predict or not to predict

A tennis ball being dropped from the top of a high building will drop straight down. This is an example of something so utterly predictable that it doesn't deserve any kind of speculation. It is simply a fact, an immutable law. For something to be called "the future", there has to be at least a hint of unpredictability about it. Demography is a bit like dropping tennis balls, in that we have a reasonably good idea of how many sixty-year-olds there will be in thirty years, but we cannot know what all these sixty-somethings will look like or how they will smell or dress, so demographic prophecies tend to be more thrilling than gravity in action.

The real foresight challenge, however, is the human brain itself. Take the mind of a thirteen-year-old. There simply isn't a method to predict how many ideas she will have, not even in the coming twelve months. Furthermore, these ideas will have a knock-on effect on the ideas of others and lead to even more new ideas. To quote philosopher Karl Popper: "What we know next will change what happens next, and we can't know what we'll know next, since if we could we'd know it now."

The falling tennis ball, demographic currents and the enigmatic human brain give us a scale between the predictable and the unpredictable. Yet the realization that part of the future will be unknowable hasn't stopped people from painting vivid pictures of tomorrow's world. This is to be expected. Human beings are susceptible to all kinds of nonsense when there is no one simple answer to a question. This is why the self-help aisles at bookstores are full of books promising ten-step happiness, lifelong romance and prosperous careers.

From tealeaves and fortune tellers to out-of-the-blue prophecies and oracles, the future has fascinated, captivated, corrupted, misled and frightened us for centuries. The fact that the future can be instantly invented in the head of an artist, entrepreneur or terrorist is too simplistic an explanation for us pattern-seeking humans. We want stories about reward and punishment. We want complexity where there's simplicity – "it couldn't have been a lone gunman that killed the president" – and simplicity where there's chaos – "the Freemasons rule the world".

What we want, above all, is control. Whether on an individual basis or as a society, we go to great lengths and participate in all kinds of meaningless charades – airport security comes to mind – if we gain even an inch of illusory control. Here is a sample of tools that are used to anticipate what lies ahead:[xiv]

1. Statistics

This is the method favoured by pension scheme salesmen who will point to past developments of the stock market and ask you to invest your savings based on this rear-view mirror portrait of what lies ahead.

2. Historical analogy

Drawing parallels to history not only makes you look unbelievably smart, it also simplifies the future as a simple repetition of things we've seen before. A successful pop group is simply "the new Beatles". Economic turbulence is merely "the 1930s all over again" and so on. "Ignore the past and lose an eye. Dwell on it and lose two eyes", as someone once said.

3. Scenario planning

Scenario planning is a kind of reverse storytelling where we mentally explore different kinds of outcomes. A certain city, London say, might become either an ecological techno-oasis or a nightmarish place of eternal darkness and acid rain. It's in essence a kind of intellectual acupuncture where the pressure points of different scenarios will open your mind to new ideas.

4. Asymmetries

Imagine moving from a rural village to a big city. What you see in this city will seem like the future because development and modernization are asymmetric in the world. This fourth method is simply to travel to places where tomorrow's world is being created –technological laboratories, fashion shows, Tokyo or Silicon Valley. Science fiction writer William Gibson famously argued that the future is already here but unevenly distributed, which is why futurologists and trendspotters function as foreign correspondents.

The question these methods beg is this: Can they actually tell us something reliable and true about what a year like 2046 AD will be like?

The <u>one</u> thing you need to know about futurology

There is no lack of evidence that predicting the future really works. In all kinds of fields we find people that foresaw the emergence of the PC, the stock market meltdown, the World Cup Champions or some other rising fortune or economic hardship we currently face. The predictioneers come in all shapes and sizes – from misunderstood professors and misanthropic thinkers to well-dressed politicians and even the odd octopus.

Herein lies the problem with predicting the future. Like alternative medicine, it only seems to work in retrospect. Sometimes. We cannot, in other words, consult misanthropes or octopi and hope that they will have answers about what our pensions will be like in the future. When American technology magazine Wired asked eight "visionaries" about how they "spot" the future, the answers were as follows:[xv]

- "There are four indicators I look for: contradictions, inversions, oddities, and coincidences"
- "The first thing I do is go where other people aren't"
- "I spot the things in the present that tell us something about the future"
- "Sometimes spotting the future is really a question of realizing what's now possible and actually trying it out"
- "I connect with people from different fields and different places and always use pattern recognition and peripheral vision to spot opportunities in unlikely places"

And, rather curiously, "I walk around Best Buy every three to four weeks and watch people".

What's striking in these answers is that they could just as easily have been the answer to the question "what inspires you?". This is illustrative of the fact that futurology is more useful as an art form than as a science. What kind of medical journal would ask doctors about the unique, personal ways in which they treat cancer or remove an appendix? As a matter of fact, when psychology professor Philip Tetlock in 1991 asked nearly three hundred experts to make predictions about the coming decades and studied the outcome over a twenty-year period, the results were underwhelming in that hardly any one of the nearly 30,000 predictions were correct.[xvi]

A monkey throwing darts or dice would have the same track record. This is the one important thing to remember about futurology – it doesn't work as a science. You cannot predict the future and if you do, it's only because we have been generous when interpreting your prediction. What we can do, however, is use futurology as lysergic acid diethylamide, LSD – the mind-altering drug.

Mind wide open

It has been argued that mankind's deepest driving force is to alter our consciousness. We read a book, see a movie, hang out with a friend, have sex, drink, smoke, and eat in the hope that these things will make us feel something. Thinking about the future serves the same purpose. We think ahead to explore what different actions and courses might bring us. What will my life be like ten years from now? Should I study engineering or eighteenth-century literature? Should I knock back one more rum and Coke even though it's past midnight?

One of the most simplistic models of human behaviour is called approach/avoid. It simply states that we operate on a kind of binary trajectory where we will gravitate towards the smell of freshly cut grass, barbecued marshmallows or a sweet summer kiss and away from things that, in our mind, will hurt or in other ways be unpleasant. In the case of futurology, this model doesn't really work. When it comes to the future, many people seem to be more attracted by pessimism – the coming plagues, famines, disasters and general misery waiting for us in the coming decades – than by the idea that life might actually become better tomorrow.

I should clarify that this tendency is especially clear when exploring our collective future as opposed to the personal future. In the latter case, people are often over-optimistic, believing themselves to be immune to the pain others will have to suffer – from divorce to sudden cardiac arrest . The reason pessimism about the future is seductive is that it's a shortcut to seem wise. If you claim to be somewhat worried about the future, you will seem wiser than if you blabber on about the limitless potential lying before us. You might be completely unprepared for a business meeting but the phrase "I see a few problems before we can move ahead with this" will magically transform you into someone who seems on top of things.

You can argue that pessimism on a societal level is a kind of immune system – what are the consequences of things like genetically modified foods? – but negativity often has its own private and vain agenda. The key, then, to actually opening your mind to future potential is not to fall back into the trenches of optimism or pessimism, but to be a "possibilist" – exploring what is and might become possible.

Let's explore some of the mental tools enabling us to do just that. I have decided to let form follow function in the coming sections lest anyone think there is a step-by-step approach to successfully predicting the future. Like a scattered toolbox or a disorganized library, the nuggets of inspiration can be anywhere. The mindsets presented below are designed to widen our thinking and expand the realm of what might be possible. Like a good philosopher, they seek to explore the boundary between the thinkable and the unthinkable.

The cone of possibility

You can write a two-word book about future-thinking: "Be Imaginative!". If we imagine ourselves looking towards the future, the lens we peer through is funnel-shaped, growing ever wider as we progress through time. What this means is that we simply have to be more open-minded the further ahead we look.

The next few years will in many ways resemble the present. We are not poised to see teleportation machines or Swedish football teams winning the Champions League any time soon. Yet as we go further ahead in time, the boundaries of what is possible widen and the impossible becomes possible. Take the 5 MB "portable" hard drive IBM 305 RAMAC in the year 1956. It's a one-tonne, ridiculously expensive piece of equipment, and all it could do was store a couple of digital images. Had digital images been invented, that is.

Today, people don't think twice about leaving a 5 GB memory stick behind at a conference because they have ten or more already. What was unthinkable in 1956 is now an everyday, quite boring phenomenon. Using the cone of possibility is about exploring the "what if?" of technology, of societal values and behaviours and in our own lives.

The plausibility paradox

The irony is that many of the things that sound wrong, illegal, stupid or unthinkable today might be the ones that turn out to be true – history is full of "impossible" futures like black presidents, gay pride parades or people living to be a hundred and twenty years old. Conversely, many things that make sense today will turn out to be complete fantasy.

This is especially true in the realm of technology, where the future of the past often showed us jetpack-propelled commuters or pill-based diets. The reason for this paradox – what sounds plausible doesn't come true and vice versa – has to do with the exponential nature of new knowledge. Before we have invented a new technology – like the ability to grow tomatoes the size of Pilates balls, for example – we can only imagine this new thing in a single dimension with everything else being equal – the same supermarket vegetable section but with giant tomatoes beside average-sized cucumbers.

What we struggle to imagine is the kind of effects giant tomatoes will have on behaviour, values, legislation and what new ideas will be created because of the new tomatoes. Even where the cone of possibility asks us to be imaginative and open-minded, we keep one hand on the railing and thus simplify the future into a place where most things remain somewhat similar, but where we will have access to a cool gadget or two.

The future porn trap

There's nothing wrong with cool gadgets. You can even argue that the most vital ingredient in prophecies is spectacle. We have come to expect and require a certain amount of "oohs" and "aahs" whenever the future is explored in movies and conference keynotes.

However, many future-thinkers fall into a trap called "future porn". What happens is that we become so enamoured with the stellar development of certain technologies that we believe everything in society will develop along a Moore's Law trajectory. As historian Niall Ferguson remarked: "We yearn for turning points. Just as economists have predicted nine out of the last five recessions, so journalists have surely reported nine out of the last five revolutions. Every election is hailed as epoch-making. Every president is expected to have a new foreign policy "doctrine". A minor redesign of a cellular phone is hailed by the devotees of the Apple cult as a "paradigm shift".[xvii]

When we make assumptions that everything will have changed in the future, we ignore the variable rates of change. Mobile phones might become ever more powerful, but we will still call them "telephones" and claim that they're "ringing" because language development lags behind technological development. Stock markets rise and fall in milliseconds whereas societies take decades, even centuries, to change. Some things might not change at all. We might still appreciate the salty taste of oysters, get drunk on red wine and use the word "shit!" as an expletive centuries from now. Future porn traps us into believing that we will all be living in some unrecognizable, foreign galaxy a century from now.

Clue hunting

We are doing "the future" a disservice when we believe it is a place that can be reduced to a handful of observations about transportation modes and robots. We do the past similar injustice when we learn that certain years were about only <u>one</u> thing. The year 1066, for example, was home to millions of people around the world who had greater worries and dreams than some remote battle on the English coast. A battle they probably didn't hear about until years later, if at all.

The future is a vast statue whose enormity we simply cannot fully observe or absorb. But we can, like a blind person, start patting down certain parts of the statue and imagine what it might be or look like. The way to do this is to use a method called clue hunting. It entails gathering clues as to what the future might be about. Statistics, historical analogies, scenarios and cool gadgets are great clues. They might not give the full or even the correct story, but they force us to ask new questions that make us hunt for new clues.

Take mobile apps today. They are small, cheap, single-function software programs that enable us to do silly things like make the cell phone look like a beer glass or waste a few minutes playing a game featuring a Doodle jumping around on platforms. But mobile apps also give us a clue that the mobile phone will become – and, for some, already is – the dominant computing platform.

If we also think about the magic of technological progress, then we can imagine mobile phones being everything from a handheld hospital to an artificial personal assistant in the future. We sometimes think so much about prediction that we forget that stories about the future have greater things to give us, like inspiration, opportunities for reflection and exposing powerful capabilities. It might even inspire you to create the future, rather than just waiting around for it.

Long viewing

The world's first motion picture was created in the Eastman Laboratories in the 1880s. "Monkey Shines", as it was called, is little more than blurry images with some kind of human figure flickering in black and white. Over and over again. There is nothing in these short images that reveals the fate of movie making as an art form and a billion-dollar industry. Had we been present at the creation, we would have had to imagine, not just extrapolate, what this technology was going to be capable of. This is what long viewing is about. Imagining tomorrow.

The famous architect Buckminster Fuller expressed it eloquently when he said that "there is nothing in the caterpillar that tells you it will one day be a butterfly." The challenge with long viewing is that humans, at least in societies that have a linear understanding of time, tend to place us at the end of a timeline and often believe there is little to look forward to. The Long Now Foundation in California (Mission: "To creatively foster long-term thinking") remedies this by placing a zero in the beginning of a year. This isn't merely the year 2016, it is 02016, instantly adding a ten-thousand year perspective.

Looking for clues isn't enough, however. You must also provoke and amuse yourself. The future isn't just a logical extension of the present; it is a foreign country where weird, magical, strange things *might* have become a reality. Remember, we aren't doing this to accurately predict certain outcomes; we are doing it to flex our minds to envision different tomorrows.

When I ask people about the future, they often refer to current news headlines about social media, the rise of emerging economies like China or Brazil, the habits and values of Generation Y or similar, and usually some remark about climate change. These things sound more like a random newspaper from the past week than visionary thoughts about the future. Too many people merely extrapolate the present instead of tapping into the source of imagination.

Consider that telepathy – reading other people's thoughts – used to be considered black magic only a few years ago and is now called Twitter. Science fiction writer Arthur C. Clarke said it well: "If an elderly but distinguished scientist says that something is possible, he is almost certainly right but if he says that it is impossible, he is very probably wrong."

Future-thinking inhibitors

We can simplify changes in the world to two different dimensions: horizontal and vertical.[xviii] Horizontal change is "copy-paste" – the same things get copied across nations and markets. When you come to Shanghai, it's an impressive city but it looks like New York, and is built using tested technologies like skyscrapers. Globalization is, in essence, copy-paste where more and more people own a mobile phone, watch Disney movies, sing along to Lady Gaga songs, drive an Audi badly and work nine to five. It's transformative but not surprising. Or, to be more precise, it doesn't take us by surprise. We are not seeing a new breed of humans rising in China. We are seeing the same thing – from skyscrapers to lifestyles – being replicated in more places.

These kinds of changes are predictable and, bar the odd recession denting the curve, linear in their development. Technology, on the other hand, is vertical. It enables something previously impossible to become an everyday reality. Twitter used to be called telepathy. The 5 MB hard drive used to weigh a tonne. Filmmaking and global film distribution used to require large companies with deep pockets and is now given away for free on a Samsung phone. The impossible has become possible.

These kinds of shifts are by definition very hard to explore because we tend to see "impossible" as an end state. Technology simply cannot become infinitely better than it already is. Life simply cannot go on past a certain age. Society cannot change that much. Or can it? Most people aren't ready to challenge the impossible before it has become an everyday reality. We tend to treat the future as "more of the same" – copy and paste between nations and cities – instead of "radically different". The comfort zone of the thinkable instead of the abyss of the unthinkable. If we break out of the mental shackles of the present, we face fierce resistance from our surroundings when we suggest what tomorrow might bring.

The philosopher Voltaire once remarked that "every man is a creature of the age in which he lives and very few are able to raise themselves above the ideas of their times". Take the Swedish author Carl Jonas Love Almqvist. In the late 1830s, he published a book called *Det Går An* (rough translation: *It's tolerable*). The book made Almqvist an enemy of the people. He was forced to leave his day job as a headmaster. Branded a pervert, he was the subject of public ridicule and was publicly spat at in the face by one of his critics. He fled Sweden in 1851.

What was the reason for this violent public reaction to a work of fiction? What Almqvist wrote was that it might be tolerable for a man and woman to live together without being married. What we take for granted today was a highly controversial opinion, a dangerous idea, just over a century ago. Most of us are unwilling to be Carl Jonas Love Almqvist. We smile along instead of speaking up against the injustices and plain stupid ideas we see in our midst.

If we truly want to explore the future, we need to tear down the old in order to build things anew. Flying cars and teleportation machines are all well and good, but they don't really change society in any meaningful way and can therefore not be perceived as controversial. They don't make enemies: the only sure sign that you are exploring something revolutionary.

The Revelation: Waking up to smell the future

The Nobel Prize of Medicine in 1949 had three recipients. One of them was the Portuguese neurologist António Egas Moniz, whose discovery was prized with the following motivation:

> *It occurred to Moniz that psychic morbid states accompanied by affective tension might be relieved by destroying the frontal lobes or their connections to other parts of the brain. On the basis of this idea Moniz gradually worked out an operative method whose purpose was to interrupt the lines of communication of the frontal lobes to the rest of the brain.*

What Moniz invented was lobotomy, a surgical method based on the view that the brain's frontal lobes were in essence a kind of appendix that could and should be cut off to put hysterical, chronically depressed or otherwise behaviourally challenged patients out of their, and indeed society's, misery.

This gruesome practice is, thankfully, a thing of the past today, but it illustrates a very important truth. The world of today is full of ideas that future generations will judge harshly. From playfully patting female secretaries on the buttocks and racial slurs to disproven scientific truths and unreliable technologies, the past is a foreign country. Today is tomorrow's yesterday, but trying to dissemble what ideas will be frowned upon or laughed at in the future is devilishly difficult.

We are habit-driven creatures but don't regularly question our habits. Besides, there is a sense of finality to the present. What you see here is what you get and what you will get for the foreseeable future. Questioning the present – what many perceive as normal, everyday life – can make you look like a lunatic.

This is the challenge activists face. They are fighting a battle against present practices, from nuclear waste handling to gender equality, and in doing so they are challenging the habits of millions of people. The flag-waving and op-eds of a few hundred protesters is no match for the everyday lives of the many. Waking up to the fact that something you've been doing for many years might be wrong is just too painful an insight for us to handle. Instead of swallowing the red pill, forcing us to embrace the painful truth of reality, we swallow the blue pill and its convenient life of blissful ignorance.[xix]

The prison of the present

We assume that <u>now</u> is the norm. History often presents the past as prologue, as a neat, linear narrative that has been leading up to the present. This present holds us prisoners by making us blind to the distant past and too lazy to change the future. Convenience trumps inconvenience. The status quo can remain, well, its status. Without ruffling feathers, challenging the powers that be, and withstanding abuse, change simply isn't possible. Not the kind of deep change required to shift society in any meaningful direction.

Most of us don't even have time to reflect, let alone act. Surely the least asked question in the world today is "What am I going to do with all this free time?". Time is the scarcest resource in people's lives and we call what we do on a daily basis "business". Busy-ness. We cram our waking hours, and increasingly part of the time we should be sleeping, with all kinds of activities – ranging from the somewhat dull and mundane to the things that carry great importance to us, whether it's playing a long campaign on World of Warcraft, writing a book or silently contemplating the day over a cigarette.

The problem, as Dutch psychologist Carsten de Dreu has discovered,[xx] is that time pressure closes minds. When we are stressed, we revert to stereotypes, prejudices and other "cognitive shortcuts". Take a moment to think about the implication of this finding. We fill our life with all kinds of activities, resulting in a chronic shortage of time to reflect and open our mind.

This is problematic on a societal level, which is increasingly clear in many democracies around the world. With the majority of voters somewhat content with their lives and firmly anchored around the middle of the political spectrum, it is the extremists and radicals that set the agenda and tilt election results. From xenophobia in Europe to anti-abortion sentiments in America, we see how relatively small groups of people, willing to submit themselves to the ridicule that taking a stance entails, are governing the agenda of the more happy-go-lucky middle classes. These small groups are fighting for their kind of future, whereas the rest of us are often too stressed out by daily living to figure out what kind of future we actually want. Beyond a future that is, more or less, like today.

Infobesity

I suffer from an affliction called *fomo* or "fear of missing out". I check my e-mail first thing in the morning and sometimes in the middle of the night. I occasionally, and alarmingly, find myself spending more time watching a computer screen for news or tweets than watching my children playing.

I don't believe I'm the only fomo-sufferer in the world. The zettabytes currently flowing through the world wide web have transformed information from a scarce resource into an abundant one and, in turn, changed us from being periodic media consumers to constantly drip-feeding ourselves information. Just like eating too much fatty, sugary food is bad for you, "infobesity" can distort your perception of reality. If we really want to understand the world, we should change our information diet.

Take news, for example – or "nows", as it should really be called. It tends to be emotionally captivating and dramatic but not particularly informative when it comes to long-term shifts. Let us use homicide as an illustration of this.

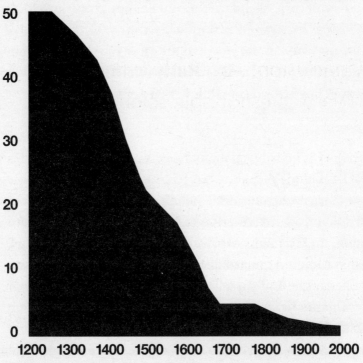

Number of murders per 1,000 inhabitants in the UK, years 1200–2000.
Source: Matt Ridley, *The Rational Optimist*.

This diagram is of UK homicide levels in the past nine centuries. What it – and diagrams from many other countries – shows is that deadly violence has declined by roughly 90% since the 1200s. Today, murder is so rare that when it happens, it usually creates big headlines, but they say very little about where the world at large is heading.

As Polish aphorist Stanislaw Jerzy Lec more eloquently put it: "The window to the world can be covered by a newspaper." In turbulent times, we would do better to look at the horizon than to stare at the waves.

Conclusion: Arguably a fine art but a very questionable science

History is invisible. It might be engraved in the memories of the elderly or hiding out in a museum or library near you. But it remains a whisper among the cluttered voices of the present. Similarly, the future is an idea waiting to happen. We might explore what this idea is capable of, but we cannot touch it until it shares our cell in the prison of the present.

This is why anyone claiming to have the gift of prophesy is a liar. They might have ideas about what shape tomorrow will have, and some of those ideas might turn out to be similar to reality when tomorrow comes. That, however, is not because of some mutation of our visual cortex, but because our thinking is free and imaginative. The author H.G. Wells, whose imaginary writings about the future made him a prophet of sorts, put it this way:

I have no crystal in which I gaze, and no clairvoyance.
I just draw inferences from facts in common knowledge.

Some of the inferences have been lucky. ... The effect of reality is easily produced. One jerks in one or two little unexpected gadgets or so, and the trick is done. It is a trick.[xxi]

These tricks of the mind sometimes play tricks on us, however. Whether we plan for our vacation or speculate about what London might be like in the year 2072, we fall into some common traps. The next chapter will explore what these traps are and how we can avoid them when practising futurology.

CHAPTER FOUR

FUTUROLOGICAL FALLACIES AND PREDICTIVE PITFALLS

"Prediction is very difficult, especially about the future."
Niels Bohr

Once upon a future...

The world was supposed to end on May 21, 2011 according to American Christian radio broadcaster Harold Camping, and the media – due to a lack of truly newsworthy material – picked it up. I attended an End Of The World Party in Stockholm that Saturday and literally partied like there was no tomorrow. The closest I came to a rapture was next morning's hangover; a trivial consequence of a severe misprediction.

Usually, we are not so lucky. We invest our savings based on broad statements about a financially bright future. We sacrifice our prime years to marry someone who promised they would always love us. We book or cancel holidays based on the advice of meteorologists. We vote based on thoughts or feelings about which candidate promises the best kind of future. We live in a prediction-addicted society and many, even most, of the predictions turn out to be useless.

The question we must ask is: why do so many prophecies turn out to be false? If we put baseless statements about Judgment Day and similar aside, what patterns can we trace in the well-intentioned misjudgements about tomorrow? This chapter will focus on six common errors in prediction – six futurological fallacies – and we will start by looking at a deep, uniquely human yearning.

Fallacy number one:
The future will have meaning

If I take a moment to think about my own future, a depressing fact becomes obvious. To quote the tagline for the final season of TV series *Six Feet Under*: "Everyone. Everything. Everywhere. Ends." All that we are in life – from the dreams we have had, the knowledge we have acquired, the homes we have built and all those we have loved – will one day be gone. In some – arguably rare – cases, our name might be engraved on an old statue, a building or the back of a book. Most of us will not even be a memory a century from now.

Our remedy is that we spend life in pursuit of some kind of meaning, and the future is a perfect companion in this quest. The future, in front of us like some majestic void, cannot answer back when we plaster all kinds of dreams, nightmares and wishes all over it. The secret deal we make is that the future will be meaningful.

Like a good story, it will make sense and provide a dénouement – a resolution to the tangled loose threads that make up the present. The bad guys will get punished. The noble will get rewarded. The meek inherit the earth.

The future, not as a place on a timeline but as a story; and like the fairy tales of the Brothers Grimm, these narratives about the future are often frightening moral fables. Revenge is a common topic – what we have built up eventually gets even with us, especially if we tamper with Mother Nature.

Punishing hubris is another favourite, currently seen in the so-called Declinist Movement. Declinism is a deterministic idea about the inevitable decline of The West/the US compared to BRIC-nations and other emerging markets. Whereas the growth of economies and the fall of poverty are things to be celebrated, many see the world as a zero sum game where the rise of one nation can only happen if another one falls. Facts get sacrificed to stay true to the Declinist narrative.

A fascinating example is Amy Chua's book on parenting, *Battle Hymn of The Tiger Mother*. Launched in 2011 as part of a discussion on the decline of the west and the rise of China and other emerging markets, Chua – a US law professor of Chinese origin – scolds US parents for spoiling their kids while promoting her own brand of Caligula-esque parenthood. She expects her young daughters to obey, study hard and rehearse musical instruments instead of wasting time on such trivial matters like sleepovers.

As expected, the book whipped up a storm in the US media – translating, of course, to stellar book sales. However, when the book was to be translated and released to the Chinese market, Chua faced a problem.

You couldn't really create the same kind of frenzied PR by telling the Chinese how their way of raising children was the right way compared with Americans. The remedy was simple. In China, *Battle Hymn of The Tiger Mother* was simply sold with the reversed message. Standing with a US flag as a backdrop on the cover, Chua was now telling Chinese parents that this was how she was raising her kids in the US, so China beware.

There are countless examples of how we try to mould the future into a meaningful narrative. Every year around December, magazines and newspapers feature predictions for the coming year. Ranging from the set calendar dates ("The Olympic Games will happen in August") to wishful thinking ("This is the year we finally embrace environmentalism"), what is striking is that many predictions made about the coming year tend to look more like New Year's resolutions. Consumers will become kinder, gentler and more ethical. Happiness will become the true measurement of progress. People will be magically transformed by technology. We will make the first steps to a carbon-neutral world. And so on.

The fact that a year is a completely man-made fabrication decoupled from how and when things happen in the real world is a moot point. The purpose of predicting the year ahead is a kind of ritual. We wash away the year that has been and whatever weight gains and value destruction it brought to focus on the pristine blank sheet of paper that we imagine the New Year to be.

When we make long-term predictions, the yearning for

meaning becomes even stronger. We use our children as tools with which to scare ourselves. What will life be like for them if we don't (limit the time spent playing computer games/ improve our schools/ plant more trees/ fill in the blank)? Children are either creative geniuses and digital natives who will put right all that we did wrong, or they are a bunch of losers doomed to live in a world of more pollution, fewer biological species, mass unemployment and a self-induced stupidity from watching too many YouTube videos.

Any self-respecting xenophobic populist politician – of the kind who tend to appear when the economy is somewhat strained, as was the case in the 1930s and the 2010s – will always reduce the future to a simple choice. Either we accept the complex, contradictory, often meaningless world we see before us, or we blame it all on the immigrants. One simple solution. One step away from a bright future. Confusion masquerading as conviction.

Fallacy number two:
The future is binary

Optimists fall into a similar trap. Where xenophobes reduce the future to a simple choice about immigration, the optimists will herald some little-known technology as the saviour that will transform our lives into something better. Be it thorium-enabled nuclear power, the internet or space travel, future generations are bound to live a life of abundance unburdened by the shortcomings we had to suffer through.

Optimists and pessimists make the same predictive error: they see the future as being binary. Heaven or hell with nothing in between. Simplistic narratives about a coming heaven, or streamline chaotic, unrelated events and turn them into something we understand and remember. A young girl attacked and killed by a wolf for no reason is just a gruesome news item. The same girl dressed in a red riding hood and saved by a hunter is a fable to learn from. We fall into the narrative trap when we plan ahead.

Take strategy plans as an example. Many organizations fail because they focus on ideas that sound good on paper but have no relevance in reality. In the spring of 2009, I made a tour around municipalities and regions in Europe and listened to the plans these places had made to attract capital and talent – preferably of the tax-paying variety. The strategies were alarmingly similar wherever I went. From Sweden to Spain, every place wanted to be at the epicentre of organic food production or green energy or IT and other "creative industries" like film, music or theatre. These are seductive goals because they sound good. No place wanted to be at the epicentre of the porn industry. Or garbage collection. Regardless of what economic advantages porn or garbage have over solar cells or organic food, the municipalities and regions were primarily interested in telling a good story, not in the harsh realities of talent and capital attraction.

Similarly, whenever a business goes bad or an idea fails, we want to attribute this to something that makes narrative sense. It wasn't just bad luck, it was hubris that killed Nokia. And so on. There must be meaning in the failure in order for the rest of us to believe ourselves to be a little safer. What if we are wrong? What if there is no such meaning? Customer taste is fickle and sometimes changes on a whim. We liked Nokia phones but woke up one morning wanting something different.

The concept of violence strikes at the heart of this idea. In our news stories and history books, violence is often put in a context where it's a logical reaction to some kind of provocation or, at least, written off as the act of a madman. In reality, violence can strike whenever, wherever. Seemingly for no particular reason. This was the learning of the South African government.[xxii] With some of the highest homicide statistics in the world, the government gave $500,000 in 2007 to a policy group to explain why violence was so rampant in the country. The findings were disappointing to say the least. There weren't any. Apart from a clichéd list of usual suspects like poverty and guns, there was no meaningful conclusion as to why South Africa had become such a violent place.

We cannot build a meaningful portrait of the future from nihilistic findings like these. Instead, we moralize about how things will develop and add a crucial "if we do/don't..." warning for good measure. Children are powerful tools in this exercise. If we don't invest enough in education, they will become troublemakers, drug dealers or just all-round bad people. If we do invest in them, the future is a glorious place full of miraculous discoveries and a greater sense of wellbeing.

We apply a moral perspective to their choice of career, believing that engineering and the arts are noble undertakings, whereas playing poker or pursuing enlightenment through substance exploration are not. We apply the same moral perspective to death and dying. You cannot simply, as many people do, slip in the shower at home or wither away in an old people's home. Your death will be the result of something meaningful. The result of not having exercised enough, perhaps, so you keep death at bay by spending hours at a gym.

Some even go so far as believing they will die in a plane crash. Talk about a spectacular death. Instead of being lonely and forgotten at age ninety, you will go down in flames. Fear of flying is a sign of grandiose self-image.

The meaningful and binary future assumes that whatever tomorrow will throw at us will, at least, be understood by us. The future will warn us in advance. In reality, the future brings abstract, unexpected and meaningless things. Like random acts of violence, five-blade razors or the bizarre 2012 hit "Gangnam Style". To quote historian Arnold Toynbee: "History is just one damned thing after another."

Fallacy number three:
"If only..."

We tend to believe that the future is about one big thing. We hear it in statements like "The future is about digital media" or "The future belongs to Asia". This thing will either put right what is wrong today or sway us off course lest we do something. The one thing that will fix public healthcare is higher salaries for nurses. What schools need are better math teachers. What the transportation sector needs is less carbon dioxide.

There is nothing inherently wrong with simplification. We need to break down big problems into small solutions. However, believing that once we solve these grand challenges things will be fine is a self-deluding illusion. There are always unforeseen consequences. Things that look simple on the surface hide deep complexity underneath.

Imagine that someone told you in the 1980s that you would have access to the world's biggest library at the touch of a button in less than twenty years' time. Surely this invention would magically transform us into a more enlightened species. Fast forward to today and the most googled term in this Alexandrian library is a teenage pop star called Justin Bieber.

"If only we had access to the world's information" turned out to be a false hope. The "if only... then everything will be solved" mindset we apply to the future misses the crucial detail that progress is as much about taking away as it is about adding new inventions. From Pluto the Planet to Fedora hats, change is characterized by disappearances. Envisioning new gadgets and more math teachers is simple compared with imagining what might fall away in the decades to come.

Fallacy number four:
"The future is now"

"We stand before the greatest challenge ever faced by mankind." The future is now. That is to say, we believe that whatever challenges we face today will also be the ones facing future generations. For inspirational reasons, we need to feel that the challenges we face are the most important ones ever. This fallacy tends to have a linear and not exponential view of the future. When we say "in thirty years…" and add some remark about the future of China or technology, we have extrapolated and drawn a straight line into the future. Were I to extrapolate the future height and weight of my children in the same manner, they would be over twenty meters tall and weigh a tonne each "in thirty years".

We take the easy way out and imagine that the way things look and function today will somehow guide what we will see tomorrow. The unexpected or the imaginative has no place in this linear future. We also assume "all else being equal". Resources will be depleted because we will run out of new ideas. Kids born in the 1990s, dubbed Millennials or Generation Y, will remain rebellious and individualistic teenagers well into their forties. We fail to realize that as we grow older, we will change. Not just our appearance, but our personalities too.

Scientists call this failure to anticipate future change the "end of history" illusion, in which people tend to underestimate how much they will change in the future. According to research, which involved more than 19,000 people aged 18 to 68, the illusion persists from teenage years into retirement.[xxiii]

The reason we fall into this fallacy is that it elevates the present – the here and now – into something extraordinary. Now is the moment we change the game. We rise to the challenge. We come together and sing *Kumbaya*. As someone with great insight once said, the most difficult thing to predict is the present. Full of contradictions and devoid of meaning, we bless it by saying the three magical words "Now is the time..."

Fallacy number five:
A one-dimensional future

A random conversation from the future might sound something like this:

Mom: *"Can you pass the toast?"*
Son: *"Oh, here it is."*
Mom: *"Thank you."*
Son: *"...."*
Mom: *"Wonder what the weather will be like today?"*[xxiv]

You might not believe me when I point out that this is an extraordinary exchange. Mother and son are surrounded by ninety as of yet uninvented technologies. Do they care? Of course not. We don't spend every waking moment marvelling about once unthinkable new technologies like nylon, Blackberries or hybrid cars. The future – like the present – will be multilayered, a melting pot of technologies, human concerns and a plethora of ideas from different decades.

This is also what tech-laden future scenarios miss. Science fiction gets its dramatic tension from one-dimensional change. Most things will be identical to the present but robots will be our everyday companions. Or women will be unable to conceive. The future becomes a one-dimensional place where every conversation and interaction is, to a certain extent, guided by this all-encompassing big idea. The reason is that science fiction, like other kinds of drama, is about reduction. We filter out all the clutter – like random conversations about passing the toast – and focus on what drives the plot forward.

The problem arises when we apply the same myopic view of the future when planning in real life. We pin our vacation hopes to that white, sandy beach on the hotel website and anticipate that the sun, the blue sky and the sand between our toes will bring happiness. When we arrive at the real-world beach, there might be a faint smell from the paper mill on the other side of the island or a noisy disco two hotels over. More people than you have dreamt about the same beach so you find yourself wrestling Germans for the best spot every morning.

Furthermore, futuristic science fiction builds on a visual narrative and rarely on something abstract like a feeling, a sound or a smell. The future becomes a specific point in time – the year 2036 or next year's vacation – dominated by gadgets or sandy beaches instead of a continuum, a rich mosaic of feelings, thoughts, scents and ideas. The future is never just <u>one</u> thing – as it is in books, movies or political manifestos. We cannot live *with* the future on the side and drip-feed ourselves futuristic stuff when needed. We will live *in* the future.

It's an immersive experience without an off button. We will have gained new knowledge when we arrive in the year 2036 and new knowledge cannot be unlearned. It destroys old truths and works cumulatively where, for example, a new kind of building material enables us to create a new kind of concert hall that, in turn, enables new sounds to be used in musical composition. A new tool enables us to view the world in new ways, and the future we were warned about never came to be.

Fallacy number six:
Everything changes, right?

Take a moment to scrutinize the budget diagram below.

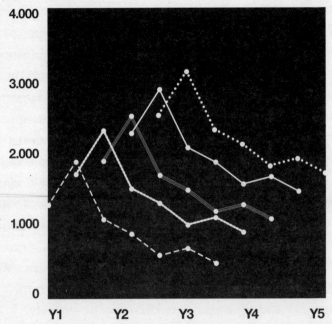

Continually revised five-year budget plans. Each curve is a new five-year budget.

I came across this diagram at a company when the CEO talked about the futility of five-year plans. What it showed was the five-year cost budgets of the past six years. Every year, the company had hoped that this would be the last year with rising costs – the hump at the beginning of the curve – to be followed by a period of frugality, cost-cutting and efficiency. Every year they had been wrong. The costs

– the starting point for each five-year plan – crept ever higher and had nearly doubled over the past five years.

We make similar mispredictions and believe that things will be different if we only give them a bit of time. We cancel lunch appointments with the words "let's try in two weeks instead", assuming that the density of our diaries or general lack of enthusiasm will have been transformed by the passage of time. Like the budget planners above staying oblivious to the root causes of the rising costs, we have a hard time envisioning the most important ingredient when planning the future: ourselves. We take ourselves out of the equation.

Psychologists have found that our natural optimistic or negative dispositions are a more powerful predictor of future happiness than specific events. They also discovered that most of us ignore our own personalities when we think about what lies ahead – and thus miscalculate our future feelings. This is why travel agencies should employ more psychologists who are able to tell us that a week at a Floridian five-star resort will be money wasted: we should go to Bristol, UK instead.

Concluding thoughts: Reducing the future

When Charles Darwin studied the evolution of finches in the Galapagos Islands, he drew diagrams of divergent lines reflecting a species that fragmented and specialized over time. Instead of unity, evolution brought greater diversity. What the pitfalls described in this chapter all suffer from is reductionism. They over-simplify and squeeze something deeply complex – the world ahead – into a cute narrative. Future-thinking becomes a movie trailer. It reduces, condenses and dramatizes in equal measures. And like the trailer for Disney's 2012 megaflop *John Carter*, reality is bound to disappoint.

Reducing the future to a few key features and feelings – whether we are talking about a technological utopia, Judgment Day or holiday bliss in the Bahamas – is seductive yet misleading. Like Darwin's finches, reality diverges and fragments. The diversity of websites, of financial instruments, of job titles and career options, of rock bands and other musical genres, and of the number of unique individuals, are all testament to this. A future-thinker's biggest enemy is poverty of imagination – a failure to think beyond the obvious and above the pitfalls described in this chapter. That's why the future of the past is a perfect illustration – not of the future, but of the past itself.

Psychologists call this "situational bias", and its implication is that when you think about the future is as important as how you think about it. Anyone who has ever woken up with a blasting hangover and uttered the words "I will never drink again" knows what situational bias feels like. To break out this bias is difficult because it requires you to overwrite whatever feelings and thoughts your brain produces in the present moment. The celebrated billionaire investor Warren Buffett proved adept at foresight when he gave away a vast proportion of his fortune with the rationale: "You tend to think clearer at age seventy than at age ninety with Anna Nicole Smith sitting on your lap."

We have a tendency to view the future as some kind of bolt-on feature to the present. Cars will have wings, robots will look like humans, computers will be better but still thought of as computers and so on. What about the things we cannot relate to yet? The unseen and the unknown? They have no place in the bolt-on future. Simplifications are understandable but regrettable.

The future isn't a place waiting to happen or a one-way street that can be reduced to a few descriptive sentences. We must avoid treating it as such lest we get incapacitated, trapped in the headlights of tomorrow. To quote futurist Bruce Sterling: "A forecast is just a phantom; it is dispassionate and unlived, unsupported by the human heartbeat of lived joy and suffering. Even the cleverest, most deeply insightful forecast becomes paper thin when time passes it by."[xxv]

The next chapter will exorcise these phantoms and shake us out of the determinism that governs many future scenarios. The role of thinking, after all, is to enable doing, changing our course, saving ourselves from colliding with obstacles on the horizon, and taking a path less travelled.

CHAPTER FIVE

CREATING AND CHANGING THE FUTURE

"Great things are not accomplished by those who yield to trends and fads and popular opinion."

Jack Kerouac

A faded dream

My grandfather, Harry Lindkvist, was an author and a rampant optimist. In the 1970s, amid the gloom that engulfed the world at the time, he published a book with the immodest title *Svaret* - "The Answer". In an informal writing style not unlike that of today's bloggers, he speculated about what wonders lay ahead of us:

> *"I am certain that what we believe can be done will be done. We will see*
> * *Risk-free nuclear energy to be used in airplanes, ships and automobiles*
> * *Solar energy will transform the developing world since the sun always shines there*
> * *Colour television will be an everyman's product and we will have a TV-telephone hybrid to see whom you're speaking with*
> * *We will overcome the language trap of Babel with automatic translation machines*
> * *Mail will be sent by rockets between the continents in a matter of minutes*
> * *Airplanes will travel at 8.000 kilometres per hour*

- *The great deserts will be greened and provide food to all people on earth."[xxvi]*

Being a man of the early 1900s, he also speculated that "every housewife's dream will come true with fully automated homes to simplify the daily chores."[xxvii]

Reading these lines in 2013, I have the sombre realization that the future lost its lustre somewhere along the way. In political agendas, business strategies and personal plans, the dreams are less grand than they were half a century ago. As writer Kevin Kelly puts it: "Excitement about the future has waned. The future is deflating. It is simply not as desirable as it once was."[xxviii]

This is not just a sentiment but a statistical fact. According to the DHL Connectedness index, the world was less global and interconnected in 2012 than it was in 2007.[xxix] Similarly, travel speeds have decreased since the 1970s due to congestion in cities and the discontinuation of supersonic passenger jets. Instead of dreaming big, many are "nightmaring" big, with one of the biggest trends in the years after the financial crash of 2008 being *Apocaholism* – wherein people stock up on gold, canned food and candles to prepare for a coming Armageddon. The future has transformed from a place of promise to one of punishment.

So far, this book has treated the future as if its primary *raison d'être* is to be on the receiving end of collective thoughts and opinions. Like some kind of eternal beauty pageant, the future is to be evaluated and re-evaluated *ad absurdum.* This is not the main reason the future exists. We are blessed with foresight to be able to plan ahead and act accordingly. It is a catalyst for action. Or to put it more eloquently with the help of Sigmund Freud: "Thought is action in rehearsal." This chapter will take a closer look at how we can reignite tomorrow by moving from future-thinking to future-creation.

Standing on the shoulders of ideas

When we are asked about the ways in which tomorrow might be different, we tend to fantasize about all kinds of cool, new gadgets and machines. From robot baristas and mobile phone implants to lightspeed-defying vessels and migrating buildings. Progress, however, does not come from new machines. On the contrary, these technologies are themselves the result of new ideas – of new mental frameworks and ways of seeing the world.

Ideas drive progress and technology is merely one of its many fruits. "Ideas" is a buzzword much loved by politicians and economists these days, so it is important to distinguish between two kinds of ideas. Between the kind that merely regurgitate existing knowledge – combining existing ideas like a cell phone, a computer and an mp3 player, wrapping it in a sleek design and calling the device iPhone – and the cognitive lookout posts that enable us to see further. The former I call horizontal thinking – it remixes elements that we already see around us– and the latter vertical thinking – we reach up and grab something previously unattainable, impossible or unthinkable.

The enlightenment, the industrial revolution and the theory of evolution were first and foremost vertical ideas that squashed old truths and created new ones. As individuals, we live in a similar state of tension between old habits and new insights, between being fenced into a narrow perspective and liberated to see the world as something bigger. If your perspective is limited by being geographically confined to a village or a small nation, you will undoubtedly draw some erroneous conclusions about who's smart and who's not or about who's rich and who's poor.

The richest man in an African village might seem like a millionaire, yet he only has fifty dollars to his name. The smartest girl in northern Sweden might be an imbecile in New York City. Cognitive lookout posts elevate our view above the suburban shrubs and we see new uncharted lands in the distance. In our daily lives, we often cede victory to habits by being in a constant state of denial. We say that living in California would not make us happier. We assume our marriage is just fine – at least compared to that of our neighbours – and that animals we eat don't suffer too much – besides, eating animals is natural, right? Our car might emit toxic fumes, but where would we be without it?

These are examples of daily activities that require a certain amount of denial to function. Were we to scrutinize our marriage, our reasons for eating meat, potential shortcomings of the combustion engine or try living in San Francisco for month or so, everyday life would become significantly harder. We need moments that break us out of denial, where cognitive lookout posts lift us up to see things from a new perspective.

When the ship Exxon Valdez ran aground and caused a massive oil spill in Alaska in 1989, Greenpeace produced the following eye-opening advertisement: "It wasn't the Exxon Valdez captain's driving that caused the Alaskan oil spill. It was yours."[xxx] Similarly, the statement "a submarine doesn't swim and an airplane doesn't flap its wings" explains the new thinking that preceded the invention of these new forms of transportation. We had to reprogramme our thinking to change our ways.

When change begins

"Magnus, you must understand that here in Norway, people aren't really into innovation and trying new things." These words came from a client of mine in the Norwegian pharmaceutical industry. It's a common sentiment, the "we-are-a-conservative-bunch-of-people" thing. I hear it in companies, industries, cities and countries. The assumption is that there is some deep flaw in these groups of people and places that prevent them from trying out new things. On the contrary, we can assume that if you are unwilling to try something new, you are rather content with the present.

Norway has the highest quality of living in the world. It is an immensely wealthy place where most individuals and companies prosper. Why would you want to rock the boat, fix something that isn't broken and experiment with new stuff if you are in a good place? The answer is that you won't. People only move when it hurts. Companies only change when they stand on a burning platform. Nations only evolve when they must. The cognitive lookout post is not some divine monolith benignly lifting us into enlightenment. It is a silent prayer in the darkest hours of night, a mirage of water in a desert, and an inconvenient promised land waiting for you when you change your ways.

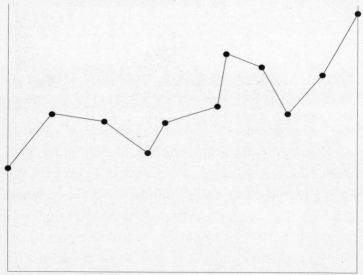

The traditional, one-dimensional idea of progress where you can only move forward and up or down.

Going forward by going sideways

The future is not necessarily a place ahead of us; it might be waiting on the sides, even behind us in time. The way we usually think about progress is as a one-dimensional, one-way curve that can go up or down.

The diagram opposite might show GDP per capita in a country in the past century, sales over a given period, life expectancy, or similar. In this single dimension, we can either grow or not grow, which is why leaders often describe their role as either pressing the gas pedal or brake, invest or save, hire or fire. However, there is another way to think about progress using a model called "Fitness Landscapes" from the world of biology.

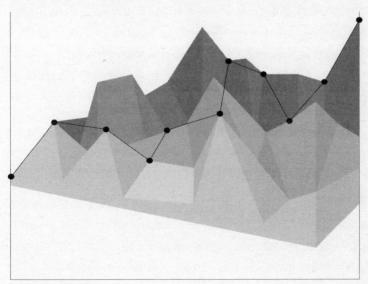

A Fitness Landscape.

In a fitness landscape, there isn't just one path towards growth. Instead, we have a landscape where an even higher peak – longer life expectancy, greater efficiency, more sales – can be found adjacently or even by going backward. In a fitness landscape, we might exhaust all opportunities on one peak so we need to climb down and sideways in order to begin anew using a different technological platform or scientific assumption.

Take the combustion engine as an example. It served us very well for a century but might be outdated in the size it requires, the noise and pollution it produces and the extractive approach to fuels it demands. To solve transportation, we need to look beyond mere energy-efficient combustion engines and reboot with a completely different approach to motorized movement. We climb down – give up on the combustion engine – sidestep in order to start a new growth cycle.

When I interviewed IBM Vice President of Innovation Bernie Myerson in 2010, his advice for people who want to become innovative was simple: "You have to know when to give up."[3] Yet giving up, climbing down, and moving sideways toward other kinds of disciplines is something companies and managers tend to be quite bad at. They prefer being competent; staying good at what they're good at rather than acquiring new, unfamiliar skills. People prefer a comfortable status quo to a turbulent unknown where the future we once held dear is lost forever.

---

3 Full disclosure: his exact words were "You have to know when to punt", but American football metaphors might be somewhat arcane to non-US audiences.

The bleeding edge

Change is weird. The moment of creation is awkward. Being a pioneer is painful. Imagine the first person to ever try an oyster. Or the first woman who ever sported a skirt. Or the first specimen whose genes mutated to produce a thumb. When something new is born, it stands out, creates friction, makes enemies and has, most probably, led to public lynching in many cases. It's safer to imitate, adapt and fit in than to aspire to originality.

Film director Lana Wachowski – who, with her brother Andy, made the phenomenally successful *The Matrix* and the artistically challenging *The Fountain* in 2006 – has the following to say about creating something unique:

> *The problem with market-driven art-making is that movies are green-lit based on past movies. [...] So, as nature abhors a vacuum, the system abhors originality. Originality cannot be economically modelled.[xxxi]*

"Innovate" and "create" have lost their value as words so that we sometimes assume they are easy. They are not. In fact, they might be some of the most difficult activities we engage in as human beings. Emulating past success, exploiting the known, is far easier and meets less resistance than exploring the unknown. And yet if we are to develop the world in a vertical, not just a horizontal, direction, we need to seek out groundbreaking ideas, lest we want the acronym R&D to mean "ripping off and duplicating" what already exists.

The diversity of ideas

The most common metaphor used to illustrate an idea – the light bulb – and the most tired examples of "good ideas" – from wind power turbines to self-driving cars – give us the impression that an idea is a thing. A thing that was waiting in the dark for us to discover it. There was a B.B.I. – "Before Birth of Idea", where you wandered in the dark looking for a solution – and an A.B.I. – "After Birth of Idea", when a stroke of insight and loud "Eureka!" heralded the arrival of a solution.

"Light bulb ideas" tend to have *one* clearly identifiable creator and owner – often with a TED-talk friendly story about how they struggled to come up with this undoubtedly brilliant, world-bettering new device. In the real world, ideas and how they emerge are as diverse as human beings. Some were individually created. Others were the result of collective thinking. Some were good. Some were bad. Some were thought to be good but turned out to be bad. Others were stillborn.

The "narrativistic" model we ascribe to light bulb ideas makes it look like there is a single, easily transferable skillset to come up with ideas. More alarmingly, we turn a blind eye to the many struggles needed to make the idea come alive. In B.B.I.-A.B.I. stories, we use moments of adversity to strengthen the narrative of creation, but the stories are told with the unfair advantage of knowing the ending. Hearing about a now famous inventor being denied a patent or about The Beatles rejected by a record company makes us chuckle, smug in the knowledge that it will all end well for Alexander Graham Bell and the Liverpudlian quartet. What we ignore is the inventors' lives before they found a solution. Lonely, poor, ridiculed or, more likely, wholly ignored and self-doubting. Stories exist for the sake of storytelling. Reality has no red thread. It is cluttered, contradictory and nihilistic.

From blueprints to recipes

In a simple, one-dimensional world where x always leads to y, we can rely on blueprints and view ourselves as architects. We can formulate a clear vision of what we want to achieve, draw detailed sketches and then formulate a step-by-step plan of how it will be executed. Once upon a time, this was how we lived our lives. Your whole existence was preordained by where you were born and to whom. The world has changed.

Today, we should use the metaphor of recipes and gardeners.[xxxii] A recipe differs from a blueprint in a number of ways. They both have a goal and a process of achieving it, but the blueprint leaves nothing to chance. You don't hope for the best when adding the last floor to a skyscraper. With recipes, you often do. The soufflé might collapse at the last moment. The whipped cream gets whisked too hard. So you need to start again. Recipes are open-ended and allow for the chance of failure that blueprints don't.

Likewise, an architect is someone who is very precise in her views on what to build, whereas a gardener will only seek to provide certain conditions in order to get things growing. If someone raises a child while wearing the architect's hat, they will lay out a very detailed plan of what that child's life should be like. As a gardener, however, they will only provide the child with some conditions and hope to watch it grow. A blueprint for life allows for no failures – you will either win the gold medal or not – whereas a recipe is a way to take chances, shrug and begin anew should certain goals not be reached.

The world of recipes and gardeners is about experimentation, a crucial skill for an uncertain future. If we have a clear view of what will happen, we do exactly what is required – we follow the blueprint – but when the view is hazy, life becomes a roulette table. Put some money on black, some on number 17, some on odd numbers, in the hope that one of the options turns out to be right. A lifelong marriage with *one* person made sense in a small, deterministic community, but in a globalized world of limitless choice, it lives on mainly for nostalgic, cultural or hopeful reasons. Hope – braving the odds – is especially important given the high divorce rates we see around the world. This is why we have seen new experiments in relationships, from the rise of dating and casual encounters to new kinds of families and constellations like one-parent households, eternal singles and same-gender parents.

The history of ideas is a constant stream of experiments.

Some succeed and become celebrated case studies. Most fail just like most mutations in the human body go unnoticed or disappear between generations. We are seduced by stories of chance encounters, serendipitous coincidences and fortunate accidents, and believe that creation will always emerge from continuous tinkering whereas most laboratory windows left ajar did not create penicillin. Most attempts to fly left people dead or injured. Most of the billions spent on R&D led to nothing and most business plans were a waste of paper. But what is life if not a faint glow of hope in an ocean of disappointment?

The fact that some, arguably minuscule proportion of accidents, mistakes, attempts and failures gave us life-saving pharmaceuticals and modern flight is reason to believe. Not that you are the chosen one, but that by doing, redoing, trying and failing, we might eventually arrive at an answer. Sometimes, we can only act by *not* thinking through all consequences.

Breakthroughs and breakdowns

In the early 1980s, the gaming company Nintendo launched an arcade game called Radar Scope that was a success on the Japanese home market.[xxxiii] Minoru Arakawa, president of Nintendo USA, therefore placed a large order to release the game widely in the US. Back then, however, arcade games were big, heavy wooden cabinets that required months to assemble and ship. By the time the game arrived in New York, months had passed and the buzz surrounding the game had died down. All of a sudden, Nintendo had thousands of Radar Scope arcade cabinets sitting unused and unsellable in a New York warehouse. He asked the game's designer, Shigeru Miyamoto, to tweak the game so it would look new and different to the American audience.

Shigeru did no such thing. Instead, he designed a brand new game that could be installed in the repainted arcade cabinets. The new game was centred on Jumpman, a chubby plumber, whose pet gorilla had kidnapped his girlfriend and was now sitting on a big tower throwing barrels that Jumpman would have to jump over to get his girlfriend back. They called the new game Donkey Kong and it went on to be one of the biggest hits in Nintendo's history. Jumpman was eventually renamed Mario after Mario Segale, the office landlord at Nintendo USA.

Today, Super Mario is one of the world's most widely recognized characters in popular culture. What we can learn from this example is the importance of recycling failures. In cartoons, a failure is simple. Wile E. Coyote simply succumbs to his own foolish plans when pursuing Road Runner and ends up falling off a cliff or getting caught in his own trap. This cartoonish storyline is often projected into the real world where politicians, CEOs, neighbours and friends are viewed as thoughtless cartoon characters pursuing some unobtainable goal. Failure becomes the logical dénouement in the quest of an idiot.

But a failure might simply be the right idea at the wrong time or the wrong execution. Think of Charles Babbage inventing the computer in the 1800s, nearly a century before it could be built. Or think of the Swedish department store *Nordiska Kompaniet* which launched the world's first series of self-assembly furniture in flat packs in the 1940s. Because people in Sweden didn't have cars at the time, the idea flopped. When it was recycled by IKEA two decades later, it became a world-changing concept.

James Joyce once stated that errors are the portals of discovery. In every work of genius, we recognize our own rejected thoughts.[xxxiv] One man's failure is another's portal of discovery. Consider the following delightful anecdote by South African artist William Kentridge about how his daughter Alice transformed an error into a miraculous fairy tale: "When [she] was about three, I was telling her a story about a cat, and the cat was being chased by a dog, and the cat ran through the cat flap and was saved. And I heard her retelling the story: 'the cat was being chased by the dog but it flapped its wings and escaped.'"[xxxv]

Innovation is a process of repeated failure until you come up with something that works. In a predetermined future, any step off the beaten path will be viewed as failure. A blank slate future works in the exact opposite manner. Only by veering can we find our own path. Only by failing can we gain valuable experience. If we never burnt ourselves on the stove or didn't feel pain when we fell off our bikes, we would never learn anything.

The corporate world is yet to master this skill. All

companies can do is succeed or fail to succeed. In success, it's champagne all around. In failure, heads roll and nothing is learned. Companies become success cults, which is unfortunate. To quote the artist Pablo Picasso, "success is dangerous because you start to copy yourself." Success becomes an enemy of innovation and progress.

Nokia, McDonnell Douglas, Laura Ashley and Sony are some examples of companies that went bad because they were good and the success made them bureaucratic, smug, failure-fearing and stagnant. Nothing fails like success and nothing catalyzes creativity more than stumbling, falling, brushing yourself off and jumping back into the saddle.

Were the Nokias and Laura Ashleys of the world stupid? Not at all. On the contrary, they were most likely very well managed if we are to believe Harvard's innovation guru Professor Clayton Christensen: "The lack of innovation is not the failure of companies but rather the result of prudent and sound management."[xxxvi] Innovation is a waste of resources given its failure rate. Sound management is the exact opposite. You want to stay frugal, conserve resources and be efficient.

Patience and persistence

"Learning from failures" has a mildly naïve ring to it in the 2000s where time has become such a scarce resource.

From millisecond stock trades to "quarter capitalism", we live in varying degrees of time-poverty. We face existential crises about where to live, what to study and what career to pursue with a sense of urgency, as if some invisible, nameless beast is chasing us. This pressure is unfortunate because time can work in our favour. Ageing can be kind to wine, art, certain kinds of music and some ideas. Time is also a prerequisite in learning, changing habits and reflection. Time, however, is very unkind to business.

A Dutch study found that the average lifespan of all companies – big or small – for the past century was a mere twelve and a half years.[xxxvii] Patience, in other words, might just be a missing ingredient of capitalism. Rodney Brooks, a businessman and inventor, had the idea of making robots accessible to consumers and households in the early 1990s.[xxxviii] The company he founded, iRobot, went through fourteen failed business models, including selling movie rights and making robot toys, before they found a suitable niche in vacuum cleaner robots.

The journey from the first prototype to a fully functioning product was a decade-long endeavour. Furthermore, the design refinements that took the Roomba from a novelty to a mass-market product took another eight years. Today, it is one of the world's bestselling home appliances – an overnight success story nearly three decades in the making.

Taking the less convenient path

George Bernard Shaw, a man of many aphorisms, once said: "Life isn't about finding yourself. Life is about creating yourself." Our journey towards the future is not a yellow brick road, but a series of difficult choices with unclear dividends. Some of these choices force you to challenge the here and now, which will certainly make you unpopular.

We tend to approach the future by dividing the future into "good" and "bad" ideas without necessarily going through the effort of in-depth evaluation. We simply feel our way forward, letting emotional reaction trump rational thinking. Sometimes our emotions lead us astray. What is considered a "good" is simply something that we approve of, something that feels vaguely familiar and that we might have seen before.

The TV shows *Pop Idol*, *American Idol* and similar talent show contests are characterized by the fact that the winners will sound like something you have heard before. Similarly, focus groups tend to reward ideas that remind us of something we already know, like and use. Red Bull, the soft drink, was a disaster in focus groups because it tasted like nothing you had tried before. This is why, to be truly creative, we must dare to make enemies. Not for enemies' sake but because having a vision of the future and acting on it will upset other people's idea of what the future should be about.

Consider the furore unleashed when someone tampers

with cultural traits like food, language or sexuality. Suggesting to a population that they must change their way of eating, speaking or accepting sexual deviation undoubtedly triggers protests, insults, hate and violence because people identify so strongly with the culture in which they themselves have been born and bred.

Sideways or onwards?

At the heart of creating the future lies a profound and painful question: Do I settle for what I have, or do I challenge the powers that be? Sometimes the choice is easy to resolve. With a dream body in mind or a fear of cancer, we force ourselves to reject a delicious donut or a relaxing cigarette break. The future is seldom as simplistic as donut-induced flabbiness or hazardous habits like smoking. Neither is it as straightforward as the present, which is why clear benefits now win over unclear benefits tomorrow.

When I ponder whether I would be happier somewhere else doing something different, I tend to fall back on the many conveniences the present has to offer. We settle for less even though we want more, but we can't bear the uncertainty of a foggy future. On a broader level, society can either go sideways or onwards. When things swing from side to side, it might appear as if the world is changing, but in reality we are just shuffling resources back and forth. Everything has already been invented so let's just divide up the proceeds.

Progress is sometimes misunderstood as simply embracing cool technologies and rejecting pessimism. In reality, it is brutal. Jobs are lost. Industries and societies are torn down. More alarmingly, power is lost, and that is truly frightening to those who have it today. The choice is whether we should merely compete – look sideways – or aim to create – move onwards. In the 2010s, it has become fashionable to talk about "a better world" and how important it is for us as human beings to strive toward it. This vague ambition can be dangerous. The Nazis were hell-bent on creating a better world. As are most religious zealots. Or right-wing tax-dodging millionaires. Or left-wing class warfare plunderers. One man's utopia is another man's hell. Many things we believed would create a better world did not. One problem is that we are often vague about how to measure improvements in wellbeing. The diagram opposite[xxxix] has a thought-provoking answer.

Improvement should be measured in time, not money. When we only need to work a few seconds for reading light, we are liberated to actually use the light for reading or do other things like relaxing, dreaming or inventing new light sources. What the diagram shows is that history is discontinuous. Over the years, the old skills and the old assumptions about the future were replaced by a new world of kerosene, electricity or light-emitting diodes. In a discontinuous world, the most important thing we can learn is to unlearn. We need to be aware that many facts

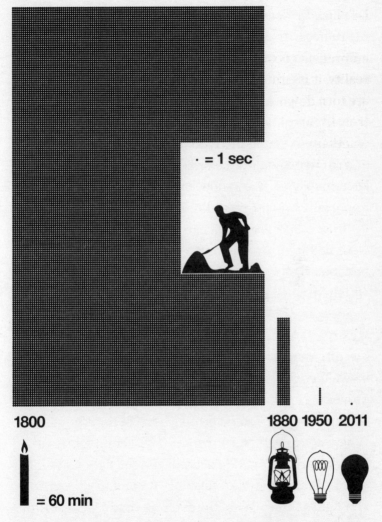

= 1 sec

1800   1880 1950 2011

= 60 min

How long do you need to work to earn one hour shown with a dot representing one second of labour. Source: William D. Nordhaus, *Do real-output and real-wage measures capture reality? The history of lighting suggests not.*

have a short half-life and need to be upgraded with new thinking. Where might the light of tomorrow come from?

I recently witnessed bioengineers – biological engineers who work with genetics to alter crops and species – who had reprogrammed the DNA of a mouse. They took a patch of genetic code from a fluorescent jellyfish and put it inside a mouse, thus enabling it to glow in the dark. When I saw it, it opened my mind to a world where the bed lamp of the future might be a fluorescent husband or wife. We should all strive to make ideas about "The Future" strange, quirky, deviant and provocative.

CHAPTER SIX
FUTURE FRIENDS AND FUTURE FOES

"Only those who are willing to risk going too far can possibly find out how far one can go."

T.S. Eliot

Stranded on a desert island

We are sitting on the beaches of a desert island of the South Pacific thinking about where to go next. Amid the sound of palm trees ruffled by a breeze, there is smalltalk about what's going on. Where are we? What matters? Did you hear about the people on the other side of the island? The island is called The Present. Surrounding this island are the shallow waters of the short-term future. Beyond lie the dark waters of The Deep Future. The Shallows can be explored by wading and looking for clues without losing touch with The Present. The Deep requires courage.

Some want to swim away from dry land and down into the darkness. Others are petrified by this thought and make arguments for staying close to shore. "We don't know what's out there." The unknown divides the group stranded on the beaches of The Present into Friends and Foes. Yet we are also united – wrong word – made equals by the dark waters of the unknown. That which cannot be known is open to whatever we make of it. "In The Deep" – the three words we use to level the playing field as we stare away at the horizon wondering about what lies beyond these shores.

The other future and the future of others

When *New York Times* columnist Roger Cohen was researching a family memoir in the early 2010s, he stumbled upon an article in his father's high school magazine from 1938 with the following passage:

> *The stresses set up by the social changes wrought by the advent of technology are straining the structure of civilization beyond the limits of tolerance. ... The machine has brought men face to face as never before in history. Paris and Berlin are closer today than neighbouring villages were in the Middle Ages. In one sense distance has been annihilated. We speed on the wings of the wind and carry in our hands weapons more dreadful than the lightning.[xl]*

A world made unrecognizable by technology and globalization was, in other words, not a concept invented by New Economy Gurus in 1999 or Globalization Savants in 2005.

So far in this book, the basic premise has been that you want to do something constructive with the time that lies ahead. In this chapter, we will reverse this assumption. Why not fear, loathe and fight the future? Every day, battles about a future – real or perceived – are being fought in town halls, boardrooms and inside our own heads. The questions are why, when and by whom the future is feared and what we can do about that.

Gravity

It is unwise to fight the laws of nature. Gravity will always be there, no matter what we think of it. Time will progress even when we want it to stop, slow down or go backwards. What we do with nature's laws is try to defy them. Just as our airplanes allow us to defy gravity, we have groups of people who try to reinvent society to reflect a better time, often influenced by the past.

The Nazi Party in Germany wanted to thrust the nation into the future by using a mix of ancient cultures, values and ideals with catastrophic results. Today, many groups in the world fight the future by offering a new Caliphate, a nation without immigrants or some other perversion of history. Extremists like these are easy to dismiss, but traces of future-fighting can be found in mainstream discourse, from heralding the benefits of local, organic food to fears of biotechnology, globalization or modernity itself. It sounds daft to fight the future, but it isn't time itself we are fighting – it is the perceived image of the future on offer.

Yesterday's tomorrow

The image we hold of the future mirrors our soul. The technological optimism of the 1950s reflected a society happy to be alive after two world wars, with a range of new inventions laid out before them, from nuclear power to plastics. The economic turbulence of the 1970s, on the other hand, replaced optimism with indeterminate pessimism, causing us to invent scenarios of a world in tatters, economically and environmentally. What we felt in the 1970s – and again in the 2010s – can best be described as *globalization angst.*

Interdependence – as globalization was known before the mid-70s – had brought benefits ranging from trade and tourism to cultural cross-fertilization. The oil shock of 1973 changed everything. As economies declined around the world, people began to fantasize about other negative side effects of an increasingly interconnected world. Apocalypse movies and zombie invasion films came of age in the 70s. As did Malthusian ideas about a planet running out of resources and scenarios of a financially and morally bankrupt western world. What we still worry about in the early 2010s was dreamt up in the 1970s.

Some dystopian images of the future function like coal mine canaries, enabling us to correct our course. More often, however, they are scare tactics used by "future-peddlers" to sway an electorate, attract donations or plant a lethal seed of fear, forcing air travellers to wait hours in security checks. The past is a useful tool when using scare tactic scenarios. We can distinguish between two reasons that the future should be feared: The Bowtie Scenario and The Diamond Scenario.

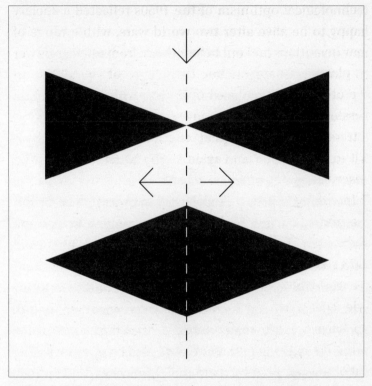

The Bowtie (top) and The Diamond (bottom). The left side represents the past, the line in the middle is the present and the right hand side is the future.

The Bowtie Scenario

The Bowtie shows the anxiety that arises from a disappearing past with the future not yet having been born. Something we cherished in the past has disappeared and we need to fight to bring it back. This sentiment is echoed on the homepage of the Silicon

Valley venture, the capitalist Founder Fund: "We wanted flying cars. Instead we got 140 characters", which reflects lost dreams of a glorious future. Nationalists use a similar line of argument when they say that national pride and glory is lost, and to bring it back we need to fight multiculturalism, immigration and culture-remixing cosmopolitanism.

The Diamond Scenario

In the Diamond, something undesirable has been growing stronger and is currently at an all time high. Here, we need to fight it back in order to stand our ground in the face of that undesirable element. Online media growing at the expense of privacy is an example of The Diamond Scenario. Or carbon dioxide emissions and rising divorce rates.

What these two models illustrate is that the future serves merely as a kind of backdrop, whereas the past is what we are really aiming for. This is sometimes referred to as the pull of the past, as if times gone by had gravitational powers, as in the closing words of F. Scott Fitzgerald's masterpiece *The Great Gatsby*: "We beat on, boats against the current, borne back ceaselessly into the past." The past is attractive. The future is unknown. The present is full of clutter and contradiction. The past is a rose-tinted memory and it is in memories' nature to feel accurate yet misrepresent reality.

Try to remember something you have experienced in life that makes you happy to think about. In my case, it would be my wedding day in June 2006. Set in Sarajevo, Bosnia, it is the closest I have ever come to feeling like a superstar celebrity. Thinking about your own happy memory, see how many of the following questions you can answer in relation to that experience:

- Who was the seventh person you met that day?
- What was the biggest news story at the time?
- How many cars did you see (make and year is a bonus)?
- What colour was your underwear?
- What time did you wake up (hour and minute)?
- What was the exact outside temperature?
- How much did a litre of milk cost at the time?

If you can answer one or two of these questions, you are truly blessed with a phenomenal memory – or the colour of your underwear was an integral part of the experience, as they tend to be on wedding days. If you can answer two or more questions, you might need to get your head examined. Memories don't dabble in details. They might isolate a detail or two – the scent of a rose, the way light reflected in the glasses, the way your uncle laughed – but they throw away all unnecessary bits and compress the remains into an emotion; in this case, happiness.

When we are nostalgic about the past, it isn't the *actual* past we are thinking about but our mental image of it. Memory is a survival mechanism that pushes people to avoid risk by applying what we've learned and relying on what's worked before. When times seem uncertain, we instinctively become more conservative – reflected in rising sales of comfort foods and the call for things like simpler banking. We look to the past, to times that seem simpler, and we get the urge to recreate them. "Life is lived forward, but understood backward," as the philosopher Søren Kierkegaard once remarked.

Living in a tense present

The 2010s are turbulent. A good word to describe them would be "flux" – things are in a state of upheaval; perhaps more so than they have been for a long time. What happens in turbulence is that we lose the future we once envisioned when things were different. Losing hurts and frightens us, so we start to invent reasons for things happening. What we don't know, we make up stories about. Gods in the clouds once caused thunder. Disease was a punishment for sin. When something bad takes us by surprise, it is natural to think about ways of preventing it.

This is why we have stop signs at intersections and urge plane passengers to keep their seatbelts on whenever seated. When unique events happen – like a psychopath shooting at innocent bystanders – we fail to take the rarity of the event into account and start regulating, as if society is full of gun-toting maniacs ready to attack at any time. It works like a ritual against what we cannot control, similar to a rain dance.

When a dozen people were arrested in London in 2006 for allegedly scheming to blow up airplanes with explosives hidden in soft drink bottles, they doomed millions of future passengers to emptying out bottles or leaving liquids behind at security. Any sane calculation would tell you that the vast majority – well above 99.99999% – of passengers have no intention to jeopardize a flight in any way, yet the symbol of airport security – security theatre as it has been called – is a ritual of reassurance. We regulate the future to prevent the past from repeating itself. The present becomes "the pressure tense", awkwardly compressed between the knowable and the unknowable. A no man's land – a no time's land – and a battleground for those who want change and those who oppose it. Those who use only the past to navigate forward, and those who believe the future can represent something new and different.

Abusing the past

Godwin's Law states that as a fierce debate grows longer and more intense, the probability of a comparison involving Hitler or Nazis approaches 100%. Future-thinker Paul Saffo once said that "you should look back at least as far as you want to look forward."[xli] This is useful when we want to get a sense of how dramatic societal change can be or how recent some things that we take for granted really are in a historical perspective.

The trap we might fall into, however, is the misrepresentation of the past in the stories we tell about it. The role of specific individuals gets forgotten or drastically blown out of proportion. Complex interconnected events get simplified to suit a narrative structure. We craft a kind of hero's journey instead of observing without passing judgment. This is why we refer to the 1400s as "The Middle Ages" when it's highly doubtful that anyone in 1421 viewed themselves as being in the middle of history. History is abused for the sake of making claims about the present and the future. George Orwell made the following remark in his dystopian novel *1984* about how inhabitants ("Party Members") of the totalitarian state are led astray by The Party:

The alteration of the past is necessary for two reasons, one is that the Party member, like the proletarian, tolerates present-day conditions partly because he has no standards of comparison. He must be cut off from the past, just as he must be cut off from foreign countries, because it is necessary for him to believe that he is better off than his ancestors and that the average level of material comfort is constantly rising.

But by far the more important reason for the readjustment of the past is the need to safeguard the infallibility of the Party. It is not merely that speeches, statistics, and records of every kind must be constantly brought up to date in order to show that the predictions of the Party were in all cases right. It is also that no change in doctrine or in political alignment can ever be admitted. For to change one's mind, or even one's policy, is a confession of weakness.

If, for example, Eurasia or East Asia (whichever it may be) is the enemy today, then that country must always have been the enemy. And if the facts say otherwise then the facts must be altered. Thus history is continuously rewritten. This day-to-day falsification of the past ... is as necessary to the stability of the regime as ... repression and espionage.[xlii]

New-o-phobia

New things, open to our interpretation, invite criticism. Tablets, smartphones and social media tools get accused of being weapons of mass distraction. Genetically modified crops are called Frankenfood. China's miraculous rise out of poverty is seen as a geopolitical risk. The science writer Steven Berlin Johnson suggested a useful thought experiment when it comes to scepticism of the new: Imagine that what is new was old and what is old is new. Imagine, for example, that the book was new while computer games had existed for centuries. We would surely have been alarmed by the isolating effect the book had on our young who – instead of engaging with communities playing *World of Warcraft* – would sit silently and watch letters on paper, without any colour graphics.[xliii]

Having worked as a speaker on trends, fads and new ideas for over a decade, I often meet resistance to new things with identity used as an excuse. Companies will look at something new and say "well, we are a big company, how is that small idea in any way relevant for us?". Individuals will say things like "we are Swedish and that will only work in the United States, not in Sweden." Identity is a barrier to change.

Think about the austerity measures in the wake of the Eurozone crisis in 2010. The Baltics, young countries with a recent history of poverty, had no problems with frugality. Greece, a rich country with a strong national identity, had significant problems with adapting to a new world. Carved into the Greek Temple of Apollo at the Oracle in Delphi were the words "know thyself." Perhaps these words were unwise. It is the identity-less person who can easily change her habits in times of change while the rest will put up a fight.

The importance of being wrong in a cowardly new world

The world wide web has liberated information flows. Knowledge can move in new directions. Hierarchies, once dependent on top-down communication, are forced to reform or perish. More people have a chance to be enlightened and, in turn, enlighten others. There is a downside, though, especially if you take the veil of anonymity into account. Ridicule, hate and all-around nastiness spread with the same ease as factually correct, useful information. Technology has, in a sense, enhanced cowardice.

As we saw in the preceding chapter, being wrong is an integral part of progress. These days, anyone caught in the act of making erroneous statements and predictions will be ridiculed, even crucified, by bloggers, tweeters and web forum hangarounds. Many have felt the brunt of this force in the past decade. If we are never allowed to be wrong, how can we ever be right? How can we ever achieve the impossible – from using new energy sources to creating new musical genres – if we don't dare to make mistakes?

To make good predictions, we must have the courage to make bad predictions. The only way to change the present is to make a brave bet on a clearly delineated future, however faulty it might seem to others. A society that functions on the basis of not upsetting others, sheltering itself from critique, will stay firmly anchored in the present. Instead of making bold predictions, future-thinkers resign themselves to vague, bland, hard-to-verify statements. We should be more afraid if our politicians, researchers, entrepreneurs and mavericks aim to please than if they attract a storm of critique. When they are attacked, we should do our best to protect them. Not necessarily their ideas, but their right to be wrong.

One for all or all for one?

Is creation the result of one – the maverick entrepreneur – or many? One enlightened individual, or the collaborative efforts of many? Followers of Ayn Rand congregate in the former camp, whereas collectivist societies like Sweden view an individual as a result of her surroundings. The Occupy Wall Street movement – a loosely organized anti-capitalist group – talked about the 99% of people (that would be most of us) versus the 1%-ers, who are supposedly made up of greedy bankers. For the Occupy movement, the idea of the few leading the many is laughable. Yet we know from history that the inventions of a few people have led billions out of poverty and out of darkness.

We pay lip service to "good ideas", but sometimes this just means that the "good ideas" are approved by society – they sound good today – but aren't good for society in the long run. Why should people with limited knowledge be allowed to make choices that require a lot of knowledge? Then again, why shouldn't they – isn't the core of democracy that even the fool is allowed to vote? The image of one person leading huddled masses into the future is offensive because we have been raised with the idea that everyone matters. From a human rights perspective, they do. But most people are not ready to make the kind of sacrifices that championing progress requires. Making enemies, wasting resources and toiling in loneliness require bravery bordering on stupidity. These will continue to be scarce qualities.

Worry, don't be happy!

"Will faster trains make us happier?" is a common question posed by sceptics where happiness is seen as a nobler unit of measurement than such trivialities as profit or percentages. Happiness is an enemy of progress. If we are happy, we don't want to change things. A world without growth would be a world where every injustice would is made eternal and no disruptions would be allowed to flourish.

Take NIMBY-ism. NIMBY is an acronym of "Not In My Back Yard", a common complaint when it comes to building new roads or shopping malls. People might be supportive of a project in general; they just don't want it in their own neighbourhood, because the specific project reflects short-term benefits whereas the spoiled view or the ravaged nature represents the long view. What if the exact opposite is true? The new eight-lane motorway would save years on annual commuting, freeing up work time. The shopping mall would provide jobs to hundreds. When we refuse to change labour laws to reflect a new reality, when we outlaw or censor ideas, the future gets sacrificed for the sake of preserving the present.

The blank slate

It became a clichéd statement post-2008's financial crisis that you couldn't predict anything. The world was now too interconnected and complex to make any kind of attempt at prophesy. Everywhere a deep pessimism about this unpredictable world could be seen, from TV series like *The Walking Dead* about a collapsed society to books about how a system-wide collapse was imminent. We were searching for answers. About the new world, its new rules and our place in it. The big leaps in understanding and moving forward are always preceded by advances in making measurements.[xliv] The microscope made us see and understand the infinitely small. The telescope made us see the infinitely large. We were now waiting for the Macroscope[xlv] that would make us see and understand the infinitely complex.

The Future – in capitals – is a destination. Armageddon or Utopia. If we view ourselves as travelling to this destination on rails, we will hate it. Like teenage kids forced to tag along to a family reunion, we will whine and make excuses to escape. Futures – plural, non-determined – are a state of mind. A blank slate and a platform to create something new or, at least, explore it in the mind. Futures are contested and contestable.[xlvi] A blank but not empty slate. Choosing sides between future friends – embracing the new – and future foes will matter more than it ever has in the coming decades. If you want to understand why, take a close look at the graph opposite:

This is the global debt to GDP ratio level of the world from the late 1800s to 2009. Someone once made the point that historians strive to give a voice to the dead.

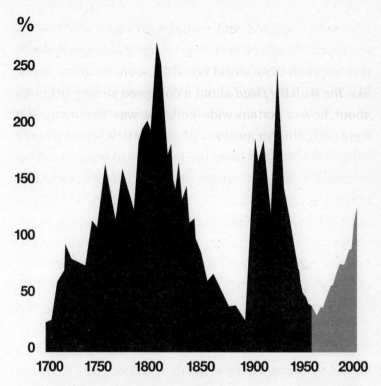

Debt % of GDP level. Aggregated for the G20 from 1950 (source: IMF, HPDD) and UK only years 1700–1950 (source: HM Treasury).

Inversely, futurologists strive to give a voice to the unborn. Debt is a promise made to future generations: "We will borrow from you to make the world that you will live in possible." When we don't fulfil these promises, all we are left with is a giant pile of money owed and no idea about how to pay it back.

The Germans have the same word for debt and guilt – *schuld* – for a reason. What we can see in this graph is the vast reduction of debt from the mid-1940s to the mid-1970s.

This didn't happen because we all became frugal Germans. We didn't shrink our way to greatness. What we had was a vision of a better tomorrow. One where we could travel faster, eat better, live longer and healthier. Not just "we". More people. Everywhere. Not everyone has the courage to create, but we should all make an effort to dream bigger and better dreams.

CHAPTER SEVEN
THE ETERNAL PROMISE

"A dreamer is one who can only find his way by moonlight and his punishment is that he sees the dawn before the rest of the world."

Oscar Wilde

A mindset for tomorrow

As I was doing my research for this book, a sociology professor approached me with the writings of a French sociologist. Her studies showed that thinking about the future is, in essence, a middle- and upper-class phenomenon. The rich are given choices. The poor are assigned a very narrow future path. This is a violation of a human right. Neurologist Oliver Sacks argues that future-thinking is a deep-seated human need:

> *To live on a day-to-day basis is insufficient for human beings; we need to transcend, transport, escape; we need meaning, understanding, and explanation; we need to see overall patterns in our lives. We need hope, the sense of a future. And we need freedom (or, at least, the illusion of freedom) to get beyond ourselves, whether with telescopes and microscopes and our ever-burgeoning technology, or in states of mind that allow us to travel to other worlds, to rise above our immediate surroundings.[xlvii]*

Like an ostrich burying its head in the sand – or should that be "in the clouds" – we long for a kind of safe haven detached from the here and now. This haven, however, has some uncomfortable side effects. With a higher vantage point, we are forced to reflect on things like our own mortality, the end of planet Earth and the possibility that our life – our relationships, our careers, our dreams – may not turn out as planned. We fill this void of uncertainty with beliefs and foresight that have many similarities with organized religion. Like a deity, we hope that the future will answer our hopes and spare us our fears. It will bring order where there's chaos. Justice where there's injustice. When we say "the future", we are referring to an intricate web of different beliefs, interpretations and intentions.

We are meaning-seeking creatures. To drift towards an unknown tomorrow is simply too frightening for many to bear. We invent stories, perform rituals and make up rules if it will give us the faintest illusion of control over the future. The convenience brought by conviction is a powerful drug. From people renouncing sex or drugs to Doomsday cults, we see that many would rather be convinced and wrong than spend their lives suspended in disbelief. What mindset should us disbelievers adopt for the future? Let me propose eight mental strategies to become a better future-thinker based on the findings in this book.

Mindset #1: Enjoy foresight

We are blessed with an ability to think ahead. It makes us worry, forces us to face consequences and scares us with images of a coming dystopia. Some people spend their lives cursing the loss of oblivion. Some see happiness only in a clueless child or in the "be here now" existence of a domestic pet. What a waste of brainpower! The gift of foresight is not a cinematic experience for us to observe; it is a vehicle of exploration. We should remind ourselves that we are lucky to have it. As my father once put it with his typical sardonic wit: "You must always take things out in advance or you might not be able to take them out at all."

Mindset #2: Be aware of the brain's shortcomings

The gift, however, is flawed. I outlined some specific examples in the chapter on futurological fallacies, but there are more. The most worrying is that we will always believe our own brain. We don't have an objective sensor for lies, slander, propaganda and unscientific hogwash. We don't automatically feel when we are wrong, so we walk around believing we are right, sometimes for an entire lifetime. We need to make an effort to climb outside the confines of our own head and into the mind of others. What secrets hide among us? What future truths will you find?

Mindset #3: Strike a balance

My grandfather Harry, to whom this book is dedicated, died in a state of disappointment. He suffered from hyperopia – living too much in the future. In the 1950s, he urged people to eat more fruit and vegetables. The diet revolution happened in the 1960s, but by then he had moved on to preaching about planting trees in the deserts of the world to save the environment. When the environmental movement came of age in the 1970s, he had moved on to championing electrical vehicles. Electric cars would suck until the 2000s, by which time Harry had been dead for over a decade. He died disillusioned with a tragic sense of not having accomplished anything in his career.

There is such a thing as dwelling too much on the future. We eagerly assume that more thinking is the answer. We are wrong. Some activities require less thinking to happen. Some thoughts lead us astray. Think about artistic geniuses with tortured souls, like author David Foster Wallace or the poet Sylvia Plath. The reason creativity and despair are often intertwined is that they both require extensive thinking.

Mindset #4: Escape the "now" trap!

Instead of asking where we are going, we should ask where we are. In posing this question, we should be careful to elevate the present to something special. We may not be in an inflection point – this is not the moment it all begins or ends, as some claim. What are we in the middle of right now? What we see around us might be part of something that began in the 1970s. Or maybe we still live in those dubiously named "Middle Ages"?

Too often, we use the present as a baseline for the future. Mobile phones are only "mobile" for those of us who remember fixed telephony. Austerity measures are more problematic for those who believed the future would only bring growth. The "unexpected" – a word often used to describe the zeitgeist of the 2010s – is really a comment about the past, not about the future. We need to stop being now-chauvinists and view time not as three different chambers – past, present, and future – but as a current flowing on many levels simultaneously.

Mindset #5: Don't judge!

We have a tendency to position the future as a problem to be solved. Instead of observing without passing judgment, we make bold claims about the need to regulate or encourage certain things. In debates about, for example, the ethics of cloning human beings, we often bypass the curious enquiry – what future benefits can this bring us? – and reach instead for the emergency break of legislation.

Similarly, when we are quick to describe someone or something as being successful, we inadvertently make them or it the maximum level of what we can achieve. An upper echelon of our imagination. To open our minds, we need to let go of Panglossian optimism or Cassandrian pessimism and instead rediscover that unprejudiced state of curiosity we once had. What is wise today is tomorrow's folly. Fashion is beautiful today and ugly tomorrow, whereas art might be ugly today yet a work of superior splendour tomorrow.

Mindset #6: Be a multicapitalist!

In November 2012, I attended a workshop where we were asked to plot our "life curve". At this particular workshop, this tired exercise had a twist. When we were done drawing the highs and lows we had encountered over the years, the moderator asked us what was on the y-axis. In other words, what unit did we use to measure our lives in? I was dumbfounded. I had rather sloppily, in a state of workshop rebellion, drawn a wavy curve without really thinking through what currency I used at the peaks and troughs I had been through.

In the world today, there are valuable things that don't have a price but should have one. Polluted waters and neglected sidewalks are known as the tragedy of the commons. There are also values that should not have a price. At least not of the monetary variety. To fully grasp and think through the plethora of possible futures, we need to adopt a greater variety of currencies and capitals, if we are to gauge progress in a more in-depth manner.

Mindset #7: Accept inequality

Not all futures are created equal. "There are some times," says chaos theorist DJ Patil, "when you can predict weather well for the next fifteen days. Other times, you can only really forecast a couple of days. Sometimes you can't predict the next two hours."[xlviii] What **Chapter Three: The Fine Art and Questionable Science of Predicting the Future** showed us is that prediction is the fool's gold of future-thinking. Some things are predictable, but that doesn't mean we should assume all our stories about tomorrow will come true.

Then we have the kinds of things that are hazy, mere shadows lurking in the fog of the future. Or the things that look deceptively close when we should never mistake a clear view for a short distance. Chris Anderson, the curator of the world-famous TED conference, said it well: "Anyone who claims to have a ten-year road map in a world changing this fast is fooling themselves. We think compass, not road map."[xlix]

Mindset #8: Think!

Your mind is unique. No two people have exactly the same thoughts and emotions in a lifetime. You should cultivate this authenticity. Enjoy the thoughts you have that nobody else will understand. Search for truths that nobody else agrees with you on. Only by exploring mental nooks and crannies can we find other, uncharted paths to tomorrow.

Leaving yesterday's tomorrow behind

When my wife, Vesna, was in her early teens she went with her choir on a tour of Denmark. It was the first time she had been away from her parents for a long period of time, so she would call home once a day. This being the early 1990s with no mobile phones, she would have to locate a nearby phone booth. A few days into the trip, the booth became unusually busy as children and teens queued up to call their parents. "You can't come home," Vesna's father told her. "You mustn't come back." There were tanks rimming the hills above her hometown of Sarajevo. My wife became a refugee of war, and although I'm grateful these events made our roads cross later on in life, I can only imagine the horror of being a father telling his daughter not to come back home because war has broken out. One future replaced by another in an instant. Visions and plans will incessantly fade with the dawn of a new day.

This has been a book about what happens in our mind when we think ahead, and what I have sought to achieve is a sense of possibility. It is easy to be cynical and simplify the future into a finite destination. To see it as something to be sculpted, a kind of destiny's clay, takes vision and courage. Vision because the future remains an abstraction. Courage because we are staring into a void and there is very little staring back. Except for our own thoughts.

The future is full of secrets, enigmas, mysteries and uncharted waters. Whether we choose to pursue them is up to us.

I write the last few sentences on 1 January and I realize what an artificial construct New Year's Day is. Every day of the year is a new year's day. Every moment is a chance to turn it all around. That should be enough for anyone to believe in that strange place we call the future. Where, as somebody far more famous than me put it, the streets have no name.

FOOTNOTES AND SOURCES

i.   This cube is influenced by a diagram created by Peter Thiel for his Stanford class CS183: Startup. Notes about the course, including the diagram, can be found here:
http://blakemasters.com/peter-thiels-cs183-startup.

ii.   This and other aphorisms of Stewart Brand can be found on:
http://en.wikipedia.org/wiki/Stewart_Brand.

iii.   A study by Klinger and Cox in 1987. Referenced on this page:
http://en.wikipedia.org/wiki/Memory_for_the_future.

iv.   Ibid.

v.   Diagram retrieved from:
http://www.economist.com/blogs/freeexchange/2011/06/growth.

vi.   Jonathan Franzen, " Farther Away", *The New Yorker*. April 18, 2011.

vii.   Kevin Kelly, *What Technology Wants*, Viking Books, 2010. Page 279.

viii.   Research cited in "The Origin of Wealth", Eric Beinhocker, McKinsey Global Institute.

ix.   Howard Schultz, *Onward: How Starbucks Fought for Its Life without Losing Its Soul*, Rodale Books, 2012. Page xiv.

x.   This anecdote was told by producer Gale Anne Hurd at a lecture in Stanford's Technology Ventures Programs. It can be downloaded here:
http://ecorner.stanford.edu/authorMaterialInfo.html?mid=2926.

xi.   Disclosed by Mr Kåre Ellingsen, of Beredskapsenheten in Oslo, at Handelsdagen, organized by Securitas on April 19, 2012 in Stockholm, Sweden.

xii.   Details of the event and the predictions can be found here:
http://www.writersofthefuture.com/time-capsule-predictions.

xiii.   Definition taken from: http://en.wikipedia.org/wiki/Futures_studies.

xiv.   Influenced by Bruce Sterling, "The Origins of Futurism", *Smithsonian* magazine, April 2012.

xv.   The article can be found here:
http://www.wired.com/business/2012/04/ff_spotfuture_qas.

xvi.   The experiment is described in Philip Tetlock, *Expert Political Judgment: How Good Is It? How Can We Know?*, Princeton University Press, 2006.

xvii. Niall Ferguson, "Turning Points", *New York Times*, November 30th, 2012.

xviii. These thoughts are influenced by Peter Thiel's Stanford class CS183: Startup. Notes about the course can be found here: http://blakemasters.com/peter-thiels-cs183-startup.

xix. These eloquent lines about the red and blue pill from *The Matrix* were taken from: http://en.wikipedia.org/wiki/Red_pill_and_blue_pill.

xx. This research is referred to here: http://www.newyorker.com/talk/financial/2011/08/01/110801ta_talk_surowiecki.

xxi. Lawrence R. Samuel, *Future: A Recent History*, University of Texas Press, 2010. Page 46.

xxii. Study described in Barry Bearak, "Watching the Murder of an Innocent Man", *New York Times*, June 2, 2011.

xxiii. John Tierney, "Why You Won't Be the Person You Expect to Be", *New York Times*, January 3, 2013.

xxiv. This example is influenced by a similar one used by futurist Bruce Sterling.

xxv. Bruce Sterling, "The Origins of Futurism", *Smithsonian* magazine, April 2012.

xxvi. Harry Lindqvist, *Svaret*, Harriers Bokförlag: 1974. Page 10. Translation by Magnus Lindkvist.

xxvii. Ibid.

xxviii. Kevin Kelly, "Futurist Stewart Brand Wants to Revive Extinct Species", *Wired*, August 17, 2012.

xxix. The study can be found here: http://www.dhl.com/en/about_us/logistics_insights/global_connectedness_index_2012.html.

xxx. Quote taken from: http://www.flickr.com/photos/_cinnamongirl_/4690971267.

xxxi. Aleksandar Hemon, "Beyond The Matrix", *New Yorker*, September 10, 2012.

xxxii. This metaphor is from Brian Eno's deck of cards "Oblique Strategies".

xxxiii. This anecdote is taken from: http://en.wikipedia.org/wiki/Donkey_Kong_(video_game).

xxxiv. This is a quote usually attributed to Ralph Waldo Emerson.

xxxv. Told at an event at The New York Public Library on March 12, 2012. Transcript can be found here: http://www.nypl.org/events/programs/2010/03/12/william-kentridge-paul-holdengraber.

xxxvi. Quote lifted from: http://virtualdutchman.com/2012/03/03/plm-kills-innovation-or-not.

xxxvii. Ven Sreenivasan, "The secret to corporate longevity", *The Business Times*, August 6, 2009.

xxxviii. This story was told by Rodney Brooks at Robotics Valley Conference, Eskilstuna, Sweden on February 9, 2012.

xxxix. Diagram based on statistics from Matt Ridley's blog post: http://www.rationaloptimist.com/blog/reader's-digest.aspx.

xl. Roger Cohen, "Time to Tune Out", *New York Times*, December 10, 2012.

xli. Paul Saffo, "Six Rules for Effective Forecasting", *Harvard Business Review*, July 2007.

xlii. Quote taken from: http://www.panarchy.org/orwell/ignorance.1949.html.

xliii. Example taken from Steven Berlin Johnson, *Everything Bad Is Good For You*, Riverhead Books, 2006.

xliv. This sentence is a direct quote taken from: http://www.news.ku.edu/2012/june/20/seizures.shtml.

xlv. The idea of the Macroscope was created by Piers Anthony. Information taken from: http://en.wikipedia.org/wiki/Macroscope_(novel_by_Piers_Anthony).

xlvi. Inspired by a quote by Cory Doctorow found on: http://fritzoid.soup.io/post/209988380/The-future-isn-t-pre-ordained-It.

xlvii. Oliver Sacks, "Altered States", *New Yorker*, August 27, 2012.

xlviii. Robert Safian, "This Is Generation Flux: Meet The Pioneers Of The New (And Chaotic) Frontier Of Business", *Fast Company*, January 9, 2012.

xlix. Quote taken from: http://blog.ted.com/2012/10/24/chris-anderson-answers-questions-like-whats-the-fairest-criticism-of-ted.

ABOUT THE AUTHOR

Magnus Lindkvist is a trendspotter and futurologist who spends his time travelling around the world to discover clues as to how we might live, work and thrive in the future. He shares these insights in his books and keynote speeches. His two earlier books *Everything We Know Is Wrong* (2009) and *The Attack of The Unexpected* (2010) have been translated into a dozen languages around the world.

He lives in Stockholm with Vesna and their twin boys Harry and Olle and can be reached on magnus@magnuslindkvist.com

ACKNOWLEDGEMENTS

No book is an island and I am grateful to all the magnificent thinkers and doers who share their thoughts – big or small – in books, blogs, tweets and magazines. I have given credit where it's necessary in this book but I am indebted to the minds of many others.

Furthermore, I would like to thank my publisher Martin Liu and his crew for putting this book together and selling it around the world.

I also had tremendous help from many friends in reading through the manuscript with Jörgen Sjöberg, Tobias Degsell, Rob Ansell and Susanna Kalitowski deserving a special mention.

Thank you, Alan Moore and Tim Harford, for the cover blurbs and your great inspiration in the books you have written.

Finally, to my wife Vesna who has had to put up with her husband being gone more than a hundred days travelling every year whilst she is being a mother and running a career as a digital marketing director. I love you and, in the end, I dedicate all my work to you and our beautiful boys Harry and Olle.

BEYOND
THE WRITTEN WORD

Authors who speak to you face to face.

Discover LID Speakers, a service that enables businesses to have direct and interactive contact with the best ideas brought to their own sector by the most outstanding creators of business thinking.

- A network specialising in business speakers, making it easy to find the most suitable candidates.

- A website with full details and videos, so you know exactly who you're hiring.

- A forum packed with ideas and suggestions about the most interesting and cutting-edge issues.

- A place where you can make direct contact with the best in international speakers.

- The only speakers' bureau backed up by the expertise of an established business book publisher.

LIDspeakers .com

Sure value.